INSIGHTS
IN DYNAMIC
PSYCHOTHERAPY OF
ANOREXIA AND BULIMIA

INSIGHTS IN DYNAMIC PSYCHOTHERAPY OF ANOREXIA AND BULIMIA:

An Introduction to the Literature

Edited by

Joyce Kraus Aronson, Ph.D.

JASON ARONSON INC.
Northvale, New Jersey
London

This book was set in 11 pt. Goudy by Lind Graphics of Upper Saddle River, New Jersey, and printed and bound by Haddon Craftsmen of Scranton, Pennsylvania.

Library of Congress Cataloging-in-Publication Data

Aronson, Joyce.
    Insights in dynamic psychotherapy of anorexia and bulimia :
an introduction to the literature / Joyce Aronson.
        p. cm.
    Includes bilbliographical references and index.
    ISBN 0-87668-568-8 (pbk.)
    1. Anorexia nervosa–Treatment.   2. Bulimia–Treatment.
3. Psychotherapy.   I. Title.
    [DNLM: 1. Anorexia Nervosa–therapy.   2. Anorexia Nervosa–
psychology.   3. Bulimia–therapy.   4. Bulimia–psychology.
5. Psychotherapy.   WM 175 A769i 1993]
RC552.E18A76 1993
616.85'260651–dc20
DNLM/DLC
for Library of Congress   93-9941

Manufactured in the United States of America. Jason Aronson Inc. offers books and cassettes. For information and catalog write to Jason Aronson Inc., 230 Livingston Street, Northvale, New Jersey 07647.

For Jay

Contents

Preface

M<small>Y</small> CLINICAL PRACTICE and my research on the level of object relations of bulimics made me aware of the multiple issues underlying therapy of the eating disorders. My teaching of psychodynamic treatment to new staff members at the Center for the Study of Anorexia and Bulimia demonstrated to me the need for a guide to the clinical literature. The purpose of this book is to make the psychodynamic literature, including its various points of view, more accessible to psychotherapists. I hope this book will be a counterweight to the enthusiasm that is so often aroused by an attractively simple dynamic, pharmacologic, or behavioral solution to eating disorders.

I thank the many people who helped me: my husband, who encouraged me to edit this book; the staff at the Center for the Study of Anorexia and Bulimia, particularly Jody Sachs, who made the library available to me; my colleagues, Ellen Steingart and April Benson, who read the manuscript and made helpful suggestions; and Diane Barth, Steve Zimmer, and Elaine Cooper Lonergan who guided me through the group therapy literature on eating disorders. I am grateful for the careful attention to every detail by Judy Cohen, the production editor; Carol McKenna, the indexer-proofreader; and Norma Pomerantz, who handled the complex task of obtaining permissions. Most importantly and indispensably, I thank the authors who generously granted permission to reprint excerpts of their work.

Joyce Kraus Aronson
May 1993

Introduction

THE ANOREXIC AND bulimic syndromes are widespread problems. They are debilitating, dangerous, and sometimes life-threatening disorders. Therapists have difficulty in establishing a treatment relationship and the patients themselves often give a history of failed treatment and many years of symptoms. An awareness of the complexity of the syndrome is necessary if the therapist is to deal successfully with the developmental deficits, family dynamics, sociocultural issues, failures in the self system, and the preoedipal and oedipal issues that account for the tenacity with which many of these patients cling to their symptoms.

This book is organized as a reference resource to facilitate access to the rich and varied literature that reflects a wide range of issues and dynamic therapeutic approaches. The extracts in each chapter are arranged by year of publication so that the reader can get an impression of the priority of observation and the growing complexity and comprehensiveness of our current understanding. The author's name and year of publication at the end of each extract leads to the original source in the bibliography.

The anorexic and bulimic syndromes represent a broad range of psychopathology. The similarity of the dramatic symptoms tends to obscure the underlying differences. Neurotic conflict, narcissism, borderline personality, or even psychosis may be present. Anorexic and bulimic symptoms can range from subtle subclinical expressions of common adolescent concerns about body image to severe starvation, leading to death.

Patients also vary in the entrenchment of their symptoms. With some, remission begins after a few months of therapy; for others the symptoms are embedded in many layers of psychopathology, and only diminish after years of developmental growth and personality reorganization. Treatment and prognosis must be determined by the personality structure underlying the symptoms in both anorexia and bulimia. A comprehensive understanding of the psychopathology is necessary to determine the indications for different therapeutic interventions.

Because many of these patients are adolescents, it is often necessary to work with parents. Even young adult patients are often enmeshed in their families, requiring treatment of parents so that the therapeutic process is not sabotaged.

Classical psychoanalytic, self-psychological, object relations, family, pharmaceutical, and feminist approaches have contributed to the understanding and treatment of eating disorders. Depending on discipline and training, clinicians tend to emphasize one therapeutic approach.

Not all anorexic and bulimic patients can be treated on an outpatient basis. Those with lower level borderline personality disorder and alcohol and drug abuse, in addition to severe anorexic and bulimic symptoms, may require hospitalization. Sometimes, however, patients with even major substance abuse problems are able to establish a working alliance, gradually give up their addictions, and engage in psychotherapy or psychoanalysis.

In practice one sees many patients who are subclinically eating disordered. Although they do not meet the *DSM-III* criteria for anorexia nervosa or bulimia, they use food to mask other problems and their bodies as vehicles for handling affect, conflict, and deficiencies in self regulation. Some of these patients have a history of more severe eating disordered symptoms in adolescence. They report episodes of bingeing, occasional vomiting and laxative abuse, preoccupation with food, thinness, and compulsive exercising.

There is marked overlap between the anorexic and bulimic syndromes. Many anorexics have bulimic episodes. Others have had bulimic episodes in the past that they are now able to control. The overwhelming majority of bulimics have a history of anorexia and bulimics who were never severely underweight report a history of wanting to lose weight. Often bulimic patients report anorexic behavior between bulimic episodes. Patients who have an eating disorder over a number of years often describe different times when the diagnosis of anorexia nervosa or bulimia could have been given. Nevertheless, the conflicts underlying their symptoms remain the same. In contrast to anorexia, bulimia as a distinct entity only entered the *Diagnostic and Statistical Manual* in the third edition published in 1980.

This is a book for browsing. The heading of each paragraph gives a quick summary of its contents. The following comments will orient the reader to the contents of each chapter.

Anorexia and Bulimia: Diagnosis

ACCORDING TO THE *Diagnostic and Statistical Manual of Mental Disorders, Third Edition (DSM-III)*, the criteria for the diagnosis of anorexia are: intense fear of fatness, which does not diminish with weight loss; disturbance of body image; weight loss of at least 25 percent; refusal to maintain minimal normal weight; and absence of a physical illness that could cause weight loss.

Anorexic behavior patterns were described 400 years before they were addressed in the medical literature. There were anorexic symptoms among female saints from the twelfth through the seventeenth centuries. This holy anorexia was regarded with awe. These women were like anorexics today, triumphantly transcending their human needs.

The first documented case in the medical literature was described by Richard Morton in 1694 — a 20-year-old girl whose illness had begun two years earlier. She refused every medication he offered and died three months later. Morton was the first to distinguish this disorder from the vague diagnosis of consumption. He called the disturbance *phthisis nervosa* a consumption of mental origin and noted the symptoms of starvation, extreme emaciation, hyperactivity, amenorrhea, and indifference to her starvation. Clinical descriptions of the disorder by Morton and later by English and French physicians in the nineteenth century are similar to those today.

The conflict between organic and psychological origins of anorexia began early. The next cases were reported by Whytt in 1767 who argued that the cause was a disturbance of the gastric nerves. Two decades later Nandeu in 1789 described a case that he attributed to the pernicious influence of the anorexic's mother. By the early 1900s anorexia nervosa was widely known and diagnosed as a specific malady of psychic origin. In 1906 Pierre Janet noted that anorexia was due to a deep psychological disturbance of which the refusal of food is but the outer expression. Yet, when seven years later M. Simmonds published autopsy findings showing lesions in the pituitary gland of severely emaciated pregnant women, medical opinion on the cause of the disorder changed dramatically. Psychological determinants of anorexia nervosa were largely ignored for the next twenty years. Anorexics were diagnosed as having pituitary marasmus. It wasn't until the late 1930s that the concept of Simmonds' Disease as a unitary physical explanation for anorexia was challenged. Even today clear, simple, concrete answers are appealing and have led to the popularity of antidepressant medication or behavior therapy as the complete answer.

Before 1940 there was an absence of comment in the literature on bingeing in relation to anorexia. This is surprising, since approximately half of contemporary anorexia nervosa patients experience bulimia as a symptom. The term *anorexia* (without appetite) is a misnomer. Its use may have blocked the recognition of bingeing. Reports of the incidence of binge eating in patients with anorexia range from rare to 50 percent. The more rigorous studies report a higher percentage of anorexics with bulimic symptomology. Most authors regard the presence of bulimia in anorexic patients as an ominous sign. Those anorexics with bulimia have been reported to be older, more extroverted, anxious, and depressed. They show more frequent use of alcohol and drugs, are more likely to be suicidal, come from less cohesive families, and have more stressful life histories.

Early conceptualizations of eating disorders precluded a diagnosis of bulimia. It was believed that bulimic symptoms existed only as one aspect of anorexia. Since 1980 attention has been given to normal weight bulimia as a discrete diagnosis apart from anorexia. Initially, bulimics were seen by clinicians as a homogeneous group with a similar underlying psychic structure.

Bulimia can be a life-threatening disorder. The bulimic syndrome is characterized by vomiting and purging, which can lead to electrolyte imbalance and hypokalemia, vascular degeneration of the renal tubules and urinary infection, epileptic seizures, chronically swollen salivary glands, and dental problems from the high acid content of vomitus. Alcoholism and drug abuse are frequent problems. Laxative abuse is often described, and is viewed by some as a sign of more severe underlying psychopathology. Some bulimics binge occasionally, while others spend as much as twelve hours a day in a repeated binge–purge cycle. The distinction between anorexics and bulimics is not as great as has been thought previously. In the '90s it has become widely recognized that some patients show anorexic and bulimic symptoms at different points in time.

Anorexic and Bulimic Range

UNDERSTANDING THE broad range of underlying psychopathology in these patients is important because engagement in therapy, establishing and maintaining a treatment alliance, and making effective psychotherapeutic interventions present different technical problems depending on the underlying psychopathology, which may range from the transiently psychotic and lower level borderline to the higher level borderline, narcissistic, and neurotic.

Bram, Eger, and Halmi (1982) documented the various levels of personality disorganization underlying the anorexic syndrome. They found a range of levels of personality organization including schizoid, histrionic, and borderline personality disorders. Patients who had a history of bingeing and vomiting showed a greater tendency to meet the *DSM-III* criteria for borderline personality disorder than those who had a history of starvation. Swift and Stern (1982) highlighted the psychodynamic heterogeneity of anorexic patients and suggested that they be divided into three major subgroups on a continuum from borderline to empty, unstructured, and emotionally conflicted. The authors emphasized that these patients range from lower to higher capacity for separation-individuation. It is only since 1980 that the normal weight bulimic is reported in the literature as diagnostically separate from the starving and bulimic anorexic.

Initially, scattered case reports appeared that described a range of severity of pathology in normal weight bulimics. Lacey (1982) differentiated three major groupings of normal body weight bulimics: neurotic, personality disordered, and epileptiform. His diagnosis of personality disorder appears to correspond to the low level borderline who require the structure of hospitalization to contain their underlying anxiety and rage. More recent literature has focused on the diversity of underlying dynamics in bulimia, reflecting what we know clinically—bulimics are a heterogeneous group. From a descriptive clinical perspective, bulimics present with a range of symptoms, such as differences in amount of bingeing and vomiting and use of laxatives and diuretics. From the clinical-empirical viewpoint, bulimics vary greatly in their capacity to engage in treatment and their response to treatment. Finally, from a clinical-dynamic perspective, bulimics represent a wide range of psychodynamic configurations that underly the bulimic symptomatology.

Countertransference

COUNTERTRANSFERENCE is an important and complex issue for the therapist. In this chapter therapists report how many of these patients, unaware of their own feelings, express them through their therapist. They use projective identification defensively, inducing feelings of hopelessness, despair, anger and guilt in their therapist, whose capacity to bear these feelings allows the patient to experience greater psychological integration. The life-threatening symptoms themselves can be intimidating and can evoke strong reactions in the therapist, who may respond with affect inhibition, hypervigilance, and counteracting out. It is essential for the inexperienced therapist to have a means of processing the affective states that may be stirred up. Supervision or participation in peer groups may be helpful.

Defending against Affect

ANOREXIC AND BULIMIC symptoms can be viewed as defenses against unbearable and overwhelming affects. Long-term clinical work reveals terror of strong affect, both positive and negative. There is a belief that

feelings will be overwhelming and burdensome to others, and will
cause rejection. Yearnings to be touched, held, or merged with others,
anger, competitive aggression, and loneliness often precede binges.
Bingeing and vomiting produce an altered ego state that gives the
patient a defensive distance from the affect. As starvation, bingeing
and vomiting are given up, the affects emerge. In the course of
treatment the patient learns to identify, contain, regulate, and express
affect.

Developmental Issues

DEVELOPMENTAL DEFICITS in early life may lead to difficulties in
modulating, containing, and expressing emotion; deficiencies in abstract thinking; and inhibition in the communicative functions of
language. The developmental (separation-individuation) process for
women is different than for men and is a major reason why women are
so much more vulnerable to eating disorders.

Dynamics

PSYCHODYNAMIC APPROACHES to the treatment and understanding of
anorexia and bulimia have paralleled the evolution of psychodynamic
thinking. Since this guides therapeutic interventions we will explore it
in some detail.

Drive Theory

The early psychoanalytic writings about anorexic and bulimic symptomatology centered on conflicts around sexuality, specifically, pregnancy wishes and fears. Falstein and colleagues (1956) were the first
theorists to bring a more complex formulation to the study of these
disorders, emphasizing that food for the anorexic symbolized part and
whole objects, feces, sexual organs, and poison.

Developmental Ego Psychology

In the last thirty years theorists have viewed anorexia and bulimia in
terms of developmental theory and separation-individuation issues.

The first two major contributors within this broad category were Bruch (1962) and Palazzoli (1963), both of whom held similar views of the major underlying dynamics of the mother–child relationship in anorexia. Bruch saw the narcissistic mother as unwilling and unable to allow her daughter to recognize her own signals and needs. The child is not valued in her own right, but as an extension of the parent. Child initiated cues are not acknowledged, and as a result, the child is not given an opportunity to know what she wants. The anorexic is unable to be constructively assertive and is condemned to a life of compliance to the expectations of others. Bruch's explanation for anorexic be-havior was faulty learning. Her formulations did not include the role of the unconscious or the drives. She disagreed strongly with the classical psychoanalysts of her day, critical of the aloof, analytic position from which intrusive interpretations were made. In her later papers, Bruch said that her views on the treatment of eating disorders resembled those expressed by Kohut in his psychology of the self, particularly Kohut's empathic response to the patient's distress and his focus on reconstruction of the developmental factors that interfered with an adequate sense of self.

Palazzoli (1963) saw the overprotective, intrusive, and controlling mother as unable to perceive her child as separate, preventing the child from deriving pleasure separately from her. This results in the anorexic's sense of ineffectiveness of thought and action and the helplessness and depression of the ego. The body is regarded as a threatening entity, invested with the negative attitudes of the primary maternal object. Because of the patient's pathological fusion of self and object representations, the body is seen as an intrusive entity whose growth must be halted.

Melitta Sperling (1955) was a classical psychoanalyst who inte-grated drive theory and developmental issues. In severe eating distur-bances, Sperling noted highly ambivalent feelings of the mother toward the patient. These feelings stemmed either from the mother's unresolved ambivalence about her own mother, which she transferred onto the child, or an unconscious identification of the child with rejected aspects of herself. Sperling observed that the anorexic uses food to reverse the early childhood situation in which mother was in control of food and life. Bulimia was seen as a change from excessive control to loss of control. Sperling noted that the anorexic's greatest fear is of losing control—gratifying impulses. Sperling's goal in simultaneous treatment of mother and child was to enable the patient to separate from the mother.

Object Relations

John Sours (1980) presented a multifaceted object relations view. He saw eating disorders on a developmental continuum of separation-individuation ranging from symbiosis to on the way to object constancy. He found developmental histories of patients within the anorexic syndrome to be characterized by parental emphasis on delay and control of pleasure. After an initial period of tolerance and sometimes overindulgence of oral gratification, the toddler is prematurely pushed to conform to a parental style that emphasizes compliance and socially acceptable behavior. Parents discourage separation and autonomy and, while adequate, take little pleasure in parenting. The child does not show oppositional behavior, negativism, and muscular exploratory activity in the practicing and rapprochement subphase. To maintain maternal approval, the child must deny wishes for separation-individuation. Mothers of anorexics tend to do little to foster interest and pleasure in the outside world or a sense of self in their daughters. A strict moral code with rigid narcissistic, grandiose ego-ideals takes precedence over the child's individual needs in a pleasureless, controlling atmosphere. Maternal supplies are only available if the child clings and acts regressively. When these toddlers attempt to separate and demonstrate aggression and ambivalence, the maternal response is withdrawal. Mothers encourage compliance; rewards are focused on early attainment of skills such as walking and talking. Sours saw intense ambition and idealism in the mothers whose children served as a means by which the mothers can maintain their own grandiosity and self-esteem. He suggested that the preponderance of female anorexics may stem from the mother's greater inhibitory response to the female child than to the male child in the practicing subphase. Recent literature suggests that the female's greater incidence of eating disorders is related to the greater difficulty girls have in separating from the preoedipal mother.

Integrating Drive Theory and Ego Psychology

C. Philip Wilson and Ira Mintz (1982) view anorexia and bulimia as two sides of the same coin. The abstainer and normal weight bulimics may have similar conflicts around aggression, dependency, relationships with people, sexual identity, and sexuality. According to these authors, anorexics and bulimics grow up in environments where parents subtly undermine their independence and autonomous growth. Parents are too strict and controlling of their child's behavior. In the bulimic, defiance is expressed through eating and vomiting; in the anorexic, through starvation. Gorging, vomiting, and laxative abuse reflect a loss of impulse control, as related to infantile wishes for closeness and security, and to discharge of aggression. Anorexics and bulimics are seen as insecure, dependent, and very ambivalently attached to their parents. Preoccupation with food and weight is used to avoid and mask real life problems. Underlying the symptoms are the problems around separation anxiety, passivity, and dependency. One clear dynamic in the majority of these patients is that they grew up feeling they never had control over the vital issues of their lives. They displace the need for control to food and their bodies.

Self Psychology

In the past fifteen years, self psychologists have made important contributions to our understanding of narcissistic issues in anorexia and bulimia. Alan Goodsitt (1983) viewed symptoms in bulimia as desperate attempts to drown out states of overstimulation and fragmentation. He proposed that much of the behavior of anorexics and bulimics can be better understood as autoerotic phenomena (like thumb-sucking)—presymbolic activities that result in drive discharge. Goodsitt noted the deficiency in the capacity for self-regulation and saw hyperactivity as self-stimulating behavior used to drown out feelings of boredom, deadness, and emptiness. He built on Bruch's view of the anorexic as having severely impaired awareness of internal feelings and sensations. Goodsitt, however, saw it not as a perceptual disorder, but rather as a deficiency in a sense of an organized inner self with specific goals and values. Anorexics and bulimics are unable to regulate self-esteem, mood, and tensions. In some cases the illness itself substitutes for the cohesive self. The anorexic lacks self-confidence. She is obedient and eager to please. Expanding on these observations, Goodsitt noted that the eating disordered patient feels a terrible sense that her body is too easily influenced and overwhelmed by external forces.

Richard Geist (1982) discussed how specific failures in empathic connectedness prevent the internalization of psychic structure in the anorexic. There is chronic faulty mirroring—repeated parental misunderstandings of the anorexic's need to be responded to and perceived in her totality as a unique person in her own right.

Another important factor in anorexia is the lack of parental availability as idealistic, soothing, calming models with whom the child can merge. These parents respond to the patient's anxiety with panic. They communicate the message that the child is helpless without them. This results in a diminished capacity for self-regulation in the patient. Alan Sugarman and Donald Quinlan (1981), who studied hospitalized bulimic anorexics, see gorging and vomiting as a defense against anaclitic depression and the loss of self–other boundaries. Deborah Brenner (1983) suggested that binge vomiting serves the specific self-regulatory function of attempting to maintain distance from the threat of experiencing a loss of self. She noted that in treatment the bulimic begins to give up vomiting when she becomes better able to affirm her own boundaries, can differentiate her feelings from those of others, and is able to assert herself. Brenner also noted the chaotic, disruptive families of bulimics, the emotional unpredictability, rages, and tantrums of their mothers, and the reenactment with food of the ambivalent relationship. Bulimics treat themselves violently in the binge/purge as they had been treated by parents in childhood.

Out of an understandable wish for simplicity in the diagnosis and treatment of eating disorders, therapists have favored one or another dynamic and focused on it, at some cost to seeing and dealing with these patients in their layered, complex, multifaceted reality.

Eating Disorders in Adolescents

THERE ARE ENORMOUS physical and psychic changes in adolescent development. Inner conflicts are easily focused on the growing body itself and previously dormant problems emerge. Although it is not unusual for adolescents in our culture to be concerned with their weight, those with anorexic and bulimic symptomatology are troubled. However, the underlying difficulties can vary considerably. Their families are unable to prepare them for adolescence and are inadequate in handling adolescent issues.

Eating Disorders in Males

ANOREXIA AND BULIMIA are underdiagnosed in males, although they are characterized by many of the same features as in women. Males with eating disorders have similar conflicts over dependency and aggression. Recent literature suggests that there is a range of gender identity problems in these males. In this chapter, case vignettes are presented to demonstrate some of the underlying issues: the need to avoid confrontation with the powerful mother of childhood, the emotional absence of the father, physical abuse, the mother's devaluation of the father, and disturbances in gender identity.

Family Dynamics

—FAMILIES OF STARVING anorexics tend to be overcontrolling, intrusive, perfectionistic, repressive of emotionality, hypervigilant in regard to their child's behavior, and highly enmeshed. Loyalty to the family takes precedence over autonomy and self-realization. Aggression is not well tolerated. Families of bulimics tend to be more disorganized, less cohesive, with greater conflict and negativity, and to have mothers who are more emotionally distant and neglectful. Parents of bulimics have greater psychiatric morbidity, alcohol and drug use, physical illness, and marital discord.

Family Treatment

IN THE 1960S AND 1970S, many family therapists believed that family treatment alone was all that was needed. Salvador Minuchin (Minuchin, Roseman, and Baker 1978) argued that strategic interventions in family therapy brought about more workable alternatives for the conflict-avoidant, overprotective, enmeshed family of the anorexic youngster. Family therapy can be useful but it is not sufficient. Therapists who have treated eating-disordered patients know that even after lengthy family treatment in which profound change in the family system has occurred, there still is a need for individual therapy for the eating-disordered patient. Family therapy by itself does not effectively alter the intrapsychic structure, character patterns, psychosexual conflicts, inhibitions, and developmental deficits.

When an anorexic or bulimic child or adolescent is in treatment, it is often necessary to have the parents see another therapist who can help them understand the nature of the illness and what they can do to help the child's progress in treatment. Parents, who often feel hopeless and helpless, need compassionate support and guidance. They need help in understanding that the patient's preoccupation with food, weight, and dieting is an attempt to control that area of her life because she feels unable to control much else. The therapist who is working with them should try to expand their capacity to empathize with the patient, to tolerate the patient's depression, aggression, and increasingly assertive behavior that often emerges as the anorexic and bulimic symptoms subside. Even young adult patients living on their own are often enmeshed and dependent on their families, requiring treatment of one or both parents so that the therapeutic process is not sabotaged.

Family work with the chaotic bulimic family is only beginning to be addressed in the literature. Since these families tend not to stay in treatment, there are only reports from inpatient facilities. These families lack rules and boundaries. Conflicts and tensions are not addressed, family histories show alcohol and drug abuse, mood disorders, physical violence, and sexual abuse. Despite these problems, there often is strong family loyalty.

Father–Daughter Relationship

ONLY RECENTLY HAS the father's role in eating disorders received much attention. Given the breadth of the anorexic and bulimic syndrome it is not surprising that accounts of father–daughter relationships vary. Patients describe their fathers as passive, emotionally absent, superficially hypermasculine, more comfortable with their daughters as little girls than as adolescents or young adults, and warm and emotional, but unreliable. Borderline pathology appears more likely to be present when fathers are unavailable. Increasingly, cases of sexually abusive fathers are being reported.

Group Therapy

FOR SOME PATIENTS a combination of group and individual therapy can be beneficial. However, the factors that lead to a high incidence of dropouts in all groups: denial, somatization, little interest in insight, and fear of commitment are prominent in the eating disorders. Since these patients are difficult to engage in groups and often leave precipitously, some therapists have been successful using short term groups to allow patients to become familiar with group intervention, and to evaluate their suitability for long term group treatment.

Hospitalization

THE HISTORY OF psychiatric hospitalization for anorexia is unfortunately characterized by manipulation, forced feeding, and coercion. These experiences reconfirm the anorexic's developmental traumas. Except for Ira Mintz (1983a), few have written about hospitalization from a psychodynamic perspective, although inpatient treatment is crucial in the management of those patients who cannot be maintained in outpatient psychotherapy. Steven Stern (1986) describes the importance of the Winnicottian holding functions of a hospital program: protective structure, empathic availability, support of individuation, reliability, and tolerance for regression. James Sacksteder (1989a) describes how an anorexic who feels out of control of her interpersonal world shifts to control her body weight. The clinical vignette shows how this pathological displacement can be modified in a dynamically oriented hospital like Austen Riggs.

Menstruation

THE THERAPIST MUST be open to the multifaceted meanings amenorrhea and menstruation can have for the same patient at different points in treatment. Sperling (1955) commented that menstruation reawakens early issues of control over the body, the drives, object relations, and sexual identification, as well as turmoil from all levels of development. Mintz (1983e) noted that the experience of menstrual flow, in contrast to urine and feces, cannot be controlled voluntarily by sphincters and therefore elicits feelings of helplessness and passivity. This in turn operates to reawaken early oral and anal conflicts over inability to control urine, feces, and people. Some anorexics and bulimics who have complied with dominating and controlling parents all of their lives silently, unconsciously exercise their own need to control at a neuroendocrine level through amenorrhea. Menstrual bleeding can represent loss and separation from the patient's childhood attachment to the maternal object. Amenorrhea can serve to deny maturation and allow the patient to hold on to a childlike self image. Thus, the symptom of amenorrhea is overdetermined and has multiple conscious and unconscious meanings.

Absence of menstruation is common in normal weight bulimics. It is unclear whether the amenorrhea is due solely to an endocrine reaction to weight loss since it may be present without weight loss. Physicians sometimes prescribe hormones to bring on the menses since there are physical sequelae such as loss of bone mass. The psychotherapist must be aware that complying with this procedure may increase conflict for the patient.

Mother–Daughter Relationship

THROUGHOUT THE literature the mother–daughter relationship is strongly emphasized in the genesis of eating disorders. Mothers have been described as empty, chronically unempathic, domineering, overprotective, and perfectionistic. Separation-individuation is more difficult for girls than for boys because of the mother's greater identification with their daughters, who are often seen as extensions of themselves. In individuation the girl must develop an identity distinct from her mother, yet identify with her mother as a female. In identifying with the mother's caretaking functions, the female child typically becomes more obedient than the male, turning her aggression toward self control. This contributes to the greater incidence of anorexia and bulimia in women.

The Patient Speaks

THERAPISTS USUALLY write and talk about their work with anorexics and bulimics in a technical vocabulary that can be at some distance from the actual situation. The patient's own words are often dramatic and poignant.

Psychopharmacology

FEW HAVE WRITTEN about the use of medication along with psycho-therapy in treating eating disorders. Yet, given the diagnostic breadth underlying these syndromes, medication may be useful in helping some patients participate in dynamic therapy. In the 1980s there was a flurry of claims about bulimia as a variant of depressive illness, treatable with antidepressant medication. But medication alone cannot change the underlying personality disorder.

Psychotherapy and Psychoanalysis

CLINICAL EXPERIENCE has shown that eating-disordered patients are a diverse group of individuals. In treating them, the psychodynamic therapist must be aware of the developmental level of the patient. Conflict theory, ego development, self psychology, and object rela-tions theory are ways therapists have found useful in listening to their eating-disordered patients and organizing the material. This chapter consists of insights from therapists writing on individual psycho-therapy and psychoanalysis.

Sociocultural Issues

SOCIOCULTURAL FACTORS have contributed to the increased inci-dence of anorexia and bulimia over the past thirty years. The cultural ideal body shape for women has evolved toward increasing thinness, not so different from anorexia nervosa. Dancers, actors, and other media role models, much thinner today than in previous decades, give teenagers unrealistic expectations about body weight and shape. The changing role of women has had an important impact on cultural expectations of how they should look. Thinness represents mastery, control, and autonomy, which become for many Americans the emblems of a safe existence. Many children are ill-prepared for the adult demands of adolescent freedom and withdraw to the only realm where they can exercise control—their own body.

Suicide and Death

SUICIDE AND self-destructive symptoms are present in varying degrees in all anorexic and bulimic patients, as evidenced in the masochistic symptoms, self-starvation, vomiting, and suppression of menstruation. When the symptoms diminish in the course of therapy, depressive affect becomes more pronounced. Some deny reality and fail to understand their own physical needs. This omnipotent thinking may lead ultimately to death.

Symptoms

EATING AS A WAY of expressing conflicts has a long and complex history. The symptom may become part of the sense of identity, a substitute for a coherently organized sense of self, or a consolation for loneliness. It can express conflicts from every developmental level and serves multiple functions. In the same patient, symptoms can be understood to serve developmental self-restorative needs as well as compromise formations. It is unrealistic for the therapist to expect patients to give up these symptoms before they have alternatives. The therapist cannot know the direction treatment will take from the initial symptom picture.

Transference

ANOREXICS AND BULIMICS are frightened of attachment and dependency on the therapist. They bring into treatment their attitudes toward their parents. This may include excessive compliance, distrust, fear of dependency, and expectations that the important others in their lives will be critical, controlling, perfectionistic, and unreliable. In the course of treatment the resurfacing of these conflicts in the transference eventually becomes tolerable, and is worked through. It is crucial that the therapist tolerate the open expression of anger, disappointment, and envy that the original objects could not.

Anorexia and Bulimia:
Diagnosis

Diagnostic and Statistical Manual-III: Diagnosis 307.10
Anorexia Nervosa

THE ESSENTIAL features are intense fear of becoming obese, disturbance of body image, significant weight loss, refusal to maintain a
minimal normal body weight, and amenorrhea (in females). The
disturbance cannot be accounted for by a known physical disorder.
(The term "anorexia" is a misnomer, since loss of appetite is usually
rare until late in the illness.)

Individuals with this disorder say they "feel fat" when they are of
normal weight or even emaciated. They are preoccupied with their
body size and often gaze at themselves in a mirror. At least 25% of
their original body weight is lost, and a minimal normal weight for age
and height is not maintained.

The weight loss is usually accomplished by a reduction in total food
intake, with a disproportionate decrease in high carbohydrate- and
fat-containing foods, self-induced vomiting, use of laxatives or diuretics, and extensive exercising.

The individual usually comes to medical attention when weight loss
becomes significant. When it becomes profound, physical signs such as
hypothermia, dependent edema, bradycardia, hypotension, lanugo
(neonatal-like hair), and a variety of metabolic changes occur. Amenorrhea often appears before noticeable weight loss has occurred.

Associated features. Some individuals with this disorder cannot exert continuous control over their intended voluntary restriction of food intake and have bulimic episodes (eating binges), often followed by vomiting. Other peculiar behavior concerning food is common. For example, individuals with this disorder often prepare elaborate meals for others, but tend to limit themselves to a narrow selection of low-calorie foods. In addition, food may be hoarded, concealed, crumbled, or thrown away.

Most individuals with this disorder steadfastly deny the illness and are uninterested in, even resistant to, therapy. Many of the adolescents have delayed psychosexual development, and adults have a markedly decreased interest in sex. Compulsive behavior, such as hand-washing, may be present during the illness. A higher than expected frequency of urogenital abnormalities and Turner's syndrome has been found in individuals with Anorexia Nervosa.

Age at onset. Age at onset is usually early to late adolescence, although it can range from prepuberty to the early 30s (rare).

Sex ratio and prevalence. This disorder occurs predominantly in females (95%). As many as 1 in 250 females between 12 and 18 years (high-risk age group) may develop the disorder.

Course. The course may be unremitting until death by starvation, episodic, or, most commonly, a single episode with full recovery.

Impairment. The severe weight loss often necessitates hospitalization to prevent death by starvation.

Complications. Follow-up studies indicate mortality rates between 15% and 21%.

Familial pattern. The disorder is more common among sisters and mothers of individuals with the disorder than in the general population.

Predisposing factors. In some individuals the onset of illness is associated with a stressful life situation. Many of these individuals are described as having been overly perfectionistic "model children." About one-third of the individuals are mildly overweight before the onset of the illness.

Differential diagnosis. In **Depressive Disorders,** and **certain physical disorders,** weight loss can occur, but there is no intense fear of obesity or disturbance of body image.

In **Schizophrenia** there may be bizarre eating patterns; however, the full syndrome of Anorexia Nervosa is rarely present; when it is, both diagnoses should be given.

In **Bulimia,** weight loss, if it does occur, is never as great as 25% of original body weight. In rare instances an episode of Anorexia Nervosa occurs in an individual with Bulimia, in which case both diagnoses are given.

Diagnostic Criteria for Anorexia Nervosa

A. Intense fear of becoming obese, which does not diminish as weight loss progresses.

B. Disturbance of body image, e.g., claiming to "feel fat" even when emaciated.

C. Weight loss of at least 25% of original body weight or, if under 18 years of age, weight loss from original body weight plus projected weight gain expected from growth charts may be combined to make the 25%.

D. Refusal to maintain body weight over a minimal normal weight for age and height.

E. No known physical illness that would account for the weight loss.

American Psychiatric Association, 1980
p. 67

Diagnostic and Statistical Manual-III: Diagnosis 307.51
Bulimia

T HE ESSENTIAL features are episodic binge eating accompanied by an awareness that the eating pattern is abnormal, fear of not being able to stop eating voluntarily, and depressed mood and self-deprecating thoughts following the eating binges. The bulimic episodes are not due to Anorexia Nervosa or any known physical disorder.

Eating binges may be planned. The food consumed during a binge often has a high caloric content, a sweet taste, and a texture that facilitates rapid eating. The food is usually eaten as inconspicuously as possible, or secretly. The food is usually gobbled down quite rapidly, with little chewing. Once eating has begun, additional food may be sought to continue the binge, and often there is a feeling of loss of control or inability to stop eating. A binge is usually terminated by abdominal pain, sleep, social interruption, or induced vomiting. Vomiting decreases the physical pain of abdominal distention, allowing either continued eating or termination of the binge, and often reduces post-binge anguish. Although eating binges may be pleasurable, disparaging self-criticism and a depressed mood follow.

Individuals with Bulimia usually exhibit great concern about their weight and make repeated attempts to control it by dieting, vomiting, or the use of cathartics or diuretics. Frequent weight fluctuations due to alternating binges and fasts are common. Often these individuals feel that their life is dominated by conflicts about eating.

Associated features. Although most individuals with Bulimia are within a normal weight range, some may be slightly underweight and others may be overweight. Some individuals are subject to intermittent Substance Abuse, most frequently of barbiturates, amphetamines, or alcohol. Individuals may manifest undue concern with body image and appearance, often related to sexual attractiveness, with a focus on how others will see and react to them.

Age at onset. The disorder usually begins in adolescence or early adult life.

Sex ratio. The disorder occurs predominantly in females.

Course. The usual course is chronic and intermittent over a period of many years. Usually the binges alternate with periods of normal eating, or with periods of normal eating and fasts. In extreme cases, however, there may be alternate binges and fasts with no periods of normal eating.

Familial pattern. No information, although frequently obesity is present in parents or siblings.

Impairment and complications. Bulimia is seldom incapaciting except in a few individuals who spend their entire day in binge eating and self-induced vomiting. Electrolyte imbalance and dehydration can occur in those below normal weight who vomit after binges.

Prevalence and predisposing factors. No information.

Differential diagnosis. In **Anorexia Nervosa** there is severe weight loss, but in Bulimia the weight fluctuations are never so extreme as to be life-threatening. In **Schizophrenia** there may be unusual eating behavior, but the full syndrome of Bulimia is rarely present; when it is, both diagnoses should be given. In certain neurological diseases, such as epileptic equivalent seizures, CNS tumors, Klüver-Bucy-like syndromes, and Klein-Levin syndrome, there are abnormal eating patterns, but the diagnosis Bulimia is rarely warranted; when it is, both diagnoses should be given.

Diagnostic Criteria for Bulimia

A. Recurrent episodes of binge eating (rapid consumption of a large amount of food in a discrete period of time, usually less than two hours).
B. At least three of the following:

1. consumption of high-caloric, easily ingested food during a binge
2. inconspicuous eating during a binge
3. termination of such eating episodes by abdominal pain, sleep, social interruption, or self-induced vomiting
4. repeated attempts to lose weight by severely restrictive diets, self-induced vomiting, or use of cathartics or diuretics
5. frequent weight fluctuations greater than ten pounds due to alternating binges and fasts.

C. Awareness that the eating pattern is abnormal and fear of not being able to stop eating voluntarily.
D. Depressed mood and self-deprecating thoughts following eating binges.
E. The bulimic episodes are not due to Anorexia Nervosa or any known physical disorder.

American Psychiatric Association, 1980
p. 69

Skeletal Appearance and Denial

THE COMMON, self-starving pattern of the anorectic is a persistent need to diet; she manages to live on no more than 400 calories a day which eventually results in generalized body wasting, sunken, glazed eyes, a cage of chest bones, a hollow abdomen, and emaciated limbs reminiscent of the most gruesome photojournalistic reports of concentration camp victims during World War II. At the same time, she denies her skeletal appearance and insists that she is still overweight. She suffers from an encapsulated madness that makes her insist that she is not ill, never felt better, and sees no reason to be cured of anything.

John Sours, 1980
p. 3

A Developmental and Psychosomatic Syndrome

IN ENGLAND, on the continent, and in the United States, countless attempts have been made to define anorexia nervosa as a specific nosological entity. The disorder has been called hysteria, obsessional neurosis, a *forme fruste* of manic-depressive or schizophrenic psychosis, a special form of psychosis, halfway between depression and schizophrenia, or an obscure organic disease of appetite regulation. Clinical evidence now strongly suggests that anorexia nervosa should be considered a developmental syndrome or a symptom-complex with its components—X_1, X_2, X_3, . . . X_n—not related to a specific reciprocal cause, Y, but, instead, to a behavioral-dynamic pattern of multiple, complex, and interacting factors. Anorexia nervosa can also be thought of as a maladaptive attempt, expressed within a range of nosological and classificatory clusters, for resolving developmental issues through symptomatic and characterological changes. Anorexia nervosa, it is clear, is a developmental and psychosomatic syndrome, which is associated with certain psychopathologies and characterological styles.

John Sours, 1980
p. 222

⊇

Body-Image Alteration Is Not Pathognomonic

THE BODY-IMAGE alteration may be commensurate to expectable adolescent discomfort, a result of denial of weight loss, or an expression of disordered body perceptions, such as found in severe borderline and psychotic patients. Whatever its nature and intensity, the distortion is only one of a number of signs and symptoms and should not be viewed as pathognomonic of anorexia nervosa.

John Sours, 1980
p. 233

⊇

A Deliberate Pursuit of Thinness

ANOREXIA CAN be defined as a conscious refusal to eat, or self-starvation, which can be so severe that it results in death. It is a deliberate pursuit of thinness, tenaciously adhered to in spite of warnings of danger by family and physicians. It is most common in adolescent girls, although it is also present in older women and has become increasingly evident in adolescent boys.

Ira Mintz, 1983c
p. 85

⊇

Fear of Being Fat

THERE IS A widespread fear of being fat in our culture. In certain individuals it develops into a phobic avoidance of food with self-starvation. When this occurs, the diagnosis of abstaining anorexia nervosa is made. In other individuals the ego structure is different; they attempt self-starvation but cannot control their voraciousness and give in to the impulse to gorge. They then try to reestablish control by vomiting and using laxatives. These are the bulimic anorexics.

C. Philip Wilson, 1983a
p. 1

כ

Pubertätsmagersucht

T HE TERM "anorexia nervosa" was coined in the nineteenth century from classical roots and has acquired the patina of historic usage. Unfortunately, the term "anorexia" is misleading, since anorexia nervosa does not involve a change in appetite in the medical sense, except when the patient is extremely ill from starvation. The term "weight phobia," often used by Crisp, describes the situation more clearly, but even "phobia" does not do justice to the syndrome, because the disorder is more complex than a phobia. The French terms, "mental anorexia" (*l'anorexie mentale*) or "hysterical anorexia" (*l'anorexie hystérique*) at least indicate that the appetite "loss" is qualified by a mental symptom. The German term for this disorder typically encompasses an entire phrase in a single word: *Pubertätsmagersucht* means "leanness passion of puberty," and perhaps describes best the essential feature of the disorder. Since no single term in English suffices, however, we are probably left with "anorexia nervosa."

Arnold Andersen, 1985
p. 35

כ

Desperate with Longing

" A NORECTIC" IS an ugly-sounding thing to call somebody whose deepest and most urgent need is to be thought beautiful. I also don't like it because "anorexia" means "absence of appetite," and except in certain specific situations, people with this condition do not lose their appetites. They are *hungry, hungry, hungry*. This term is additionally inaccurate as a description of this condition because it is derived from the Greek "an," meaning "without," and "orexis," meaning "longing." Girls with this condition, however, are not without longing. They are filled with longing, consumed by longing, desperate with longing.

Katherine Byrne, 1987
p. xii

⊒

No Good Reason to Distinguish Rigorously between Bulimia and Anorexia

THERE DOES not appear to be good reason to distinguish rigorously between the syndromes of bulimia and anorexia on the basis of psychodynamic evidence. While the symptom picture in these two syndromes can be strikingly different, and *The Diagnostic and Statistical Manual* (1980) of the American Psychiatric Association (*DSM-III*) gives specific criteria for the diagnosis of each, anorexia and bulimia may simply represent two sides of the same coin. There is no consensus in the literature that these clinical syndromes are separate illnesses, and the dynamic picture so far suggests a continuum. Some authors emphasize that eating disturbances are only symptom pictures and as such may occur in a wide spectrum of diagnoses.

Daniel Gesensway, 1988
p. 301

⊒

Gorging and Starving Are Opposite Sides of the Same Coin

UNWITTINGLY, INSTEAD of dealing with the anxiety by gorging, she would then deal with it by starving, exchanging bulimia for anorexia. In either case, she would push away the thoughts and feelings. If she felt that she could cope, she would not have to do this. Here one sees both her attempt to regulate her anxiety level by a different displacement as well as a self-destructive solution for it. Gorging and starving are opposite sides of the same coin, and illustrate that anorexia and bulimia are the same illness.

Ira Mintz, 1988
p. 147

Patients Routinely Move between the Anorexic and Bulimic Syndromes

HISTORIES OF bulimic patients reviewed longitudinally over time commonly reveal that the disorder actually began with a period of self-imposed starvation. The distinguishing characteristic between anorexia and bulimia should not be an arbitrary weight threshold but rather the presence or absence of binge eating. Patients with either disorder are overly concerned about weight and shape, but the classification of anorexia is reserved for those who have dropped 15% below their ideal body weight. Patients routinely move between syndromes at different points in time, leading to changes in diagnostic practice.

Kathryn Zerbe, 1992
p. 169

Physical and Sexual Abuse

CONFIRMED HISTORIES of sexual and physical abuse are rampant among patients with eating disorders. At any given time, more than 50% of the patients in our extended treatment unit report a history of sexual and physical abuse that has often occurred over several years. Data from the C. F. Menninger Memorial Hospital mesh well with reports in the literature that indicate a history of sexual abuse in 35–65% of these patients. However, statistics never convey the calamitous disruption imposed on the life course of these patients by very real traumas. Therapists who work daily with hospitalized eating disorder patients with a history of sustained and repeated trauma encounter a significantly high frequency of dissociative states and multiple personality disorder.

Kathryn Zerbe, 1992
p. 171

⊒

Signs of Bulimia

THERE ARE SIGNS observable on examination that should alert the clinicians to the possible diagnosis of bulimia nervosa:

1. Lesions on the skin over the dorsum of the dominant hand, resulting from the use of the hand to simulate the gag reflex. This change may be more common early in the course of the illness, since as the illness progresses patients often no longer require mechanical stimulation to induce vomiting.
2. Hypertrophy of the salivary glands, particularly the parotid glands, is common, and usually bilateral and painless. This is sometimes referrred to as "puffy cheeks" by patients. The exact prevalence is unknown, as is the pathophysiology. It may be caused by binge eating, vomiting, and perhaps excessive gum chewing.
3. Dental complications are frequent in these patients and are caused by the highly acid gastric contents leading to erosion of the enamel and secondarily to decalcification. The erosion is often particularly marked on the lingual surface of the upper teeth. The presence of erosion is related to the duration and frequency of vomiting, and vomiting at least three times a week for four years causes dental problems in a majority of bulimic patients. Other types of dental changes include increased temperature sensitivity and a possible increased rate of caries development. The rapidly developing caries is presumably related to the intake of pure sugar and foods of high carbohydrate content.

4. If examined soon after a binge-and-vomiting episode, the bulimic patient may appear flushed, and petechial hemorrhages may be seen on the cornea, soft palate, or face.
5. Other signs may include muscle weakness, and peripheral edema.

Martina de Zwaan and James Mitchell, 1993
p. 65

己

Signs of Anorexia Nervosa

SIGNS OF ANOREXIA nervosa are usually more obvious than bulima.

1. The emaciated appearance of patients with anorexia nervosa should immediately suggest the diagnosis.
2. The skin is usually dry, sometimes shows a yellowish discoloration, possibly related to increased carotene deposition, and appears "dirty." In up to 29 percent of anorectics, trunk, face, and extremities are covered by fine body hair (lanugo). Brittle hair and nails as well as scalp and pubic hair loss are common.
3. Orthostatic changes and hypotension (often below 80/50 mmHg) are very common, and the periphery is usually cold and cyanotic.
4. Body temperature (rectal temperature below 96.6F) and pulse rate (usually below 60 bpm) may be reduced. Patients with anorexia nervosa often fail to respond to cold with characteristic shivering or piloerection.
5. Other signs on physical examination may include edema (20 percent prevalence in this population) of lower extremities (e.g., pretibial), petechiae, and in rare cases pathological fractures.

Martina de Zwaan and James Mitchell, 1993
p. 66

2

Anorexic and Bulimic Range

Severity of Cachexia Does Not Correspond to Severity of Psychopathology

THE LOSS OF weight and the accompanying somatic symptoms do not correlate with the seriousness of the psychopathological syndrome. To put it another way, the severity of the cachexia does not necessarily correspond to a similarly severe psychopathology. In short, not every cachectic young girl is necessarily a severe neurotic or a borderline psychotic patient.

Helmut Thomä, 1967
pp. 439

The Broad Spectrum of Causes

ANOREXIA NERVOSA has long been considered one of the most dramatic of psychiatric syndromes. Its symptoms are idiosyncratic and its outcome potentially fatal. Because the assumed causes of this illness span the broad spectrum from neurophysiological predisposition through unconscious intrapsychic conflict to familial and cultural factors, anorexia nervosa raises fundamental theoretical questions regarding the interaction of biological and psychosocial determinants of illness.

Otto F. Kernberg, 1980
p. ix

이

Heterogeneous Developmental Disorder

ANOREXIA NERVOSA, a syndrome best defined by the patient's disturbed attitude toward food and eating, is presented as a heterogeneous developmental disorder with definite homogeneous subgroups, each with its own symptomatology, developmental background, and personality organization and style.

John Sours, 1980
p. xv

이

The Range in Expression of Symptoms Causes Confusion

ALTHOUGH ANOREXIA nervosa was described in the third quarter of the nineteenth century, it was not understood by clinicians until the last few decades. And there is still much confusion. Part of the difficulty in delineating the disturbance is that the developmental disorder ranges in its quantitative expression from minimal manifestations—commonplace teenage attitudes toward the self and the body, often fleeting and elusive—to a relentless course leading to self-starvation, cachexia, obliteration of the self, and finally death. Furthermore, the anorectic, on one end of the continuum, may steadfastly diet and starve herself to death; on the other end, she may binge and vomit in an unrelenting cycle, interspersed with periods of unnoting eating and constant weight. Then there are mixed anorectics who alternately diet, gorge, and vomit.

John Sours, 1980
p. 7

己

There Is No One Treatment

JUST AS THERE is no one anorexia, there is no one treatment for anorexia nervosa; a variety of possible, disparate therapies must be considered for each patient in terms of the basic psychopathology and stage of the disorder.

John Sours, 1980
p. 359

己

The Degree of Pathology Can Vary Greatly from Patient to Patient

FAILURE IN separation-individuation resulting from chronically disturbed parent–child interactions constitutes the core dynamic problem for the majority of hospitalized anorexics. However, the degree of pathology can vary greatly from patient to patient. For example, in the case of false self development: for some anorexics it is extraordinarily rigid and dominates the entire personality, while for others it is more a social facade, an overdeveloped persona, that does not totally constrict psychological growth. The same appears true for the degree of psychological autonomy attained by different patients. Some of the factors which may contribute to the severity of disturbance are:

1. the structure and functioning of the family, particularly the degree of pathological enmeshment of the family. It has been our experience that highly enmeshed families strenuously deny con-

flict while less enmeshed anorexic families are beset by overt conflict which they find chronically difficult to resolve. There is some evidence that the latter sort of family is associated with a better long-term outcome.

2. the habitual defensive/coping configuration of the patient, some anorexics displaying relatively "higher level" defenses — repression, reaction formation, isolation of affect, etc., while others relying totally on the "lower level" defenses, e.g., denial, projection, splitting, and turning against the self.

3. the level of narcissistic development and especially the relative adequacy of self-esteem regulation; this is particularly important to assess once the patient's weight has returned to normal since inadequate regulation may well portend vulnerability to relapse.

4. the capacity for mature object relationships, i.e. the patient's capability at maintaining whole rather than part object relationships.

5. the type and extent of character pathology displayed by the patient.

William Swift and Steven Stern, 1982
p. 20

Several Continua Must Be Taken into Account

IT REALLY SEEMS more the case that there is not one *single* continuum among eating disorder patients but rather several continuua to be taken into account. Furthermore, there is compelling evidence that there are continuua within each symptom picture, as well. Some of the areas that vary considerably *within* each category are as follows: level of pathology in areas other than the eating disorder, extent of severity of the eating disorder symptomatology itself, acuteness versus chronicity of the eating disorder, extent of ego development and/or developmental deficits (such as self and object constancy, degree and kind of impulse control, types of defenses used, and so forth), level of self–other differentiation (as well as articulation among bodily and emotional states), type and level of object relations, level of premorbid

development prior to onset of the eating disorder. Such considerations perhaps seem obvious. However, they are sometimes neglected
in the wish for simplicity and in the wish for some way of organizing
the eating disorders.

Deborah Brenner, 1984
p. 7

〿

From Schizophrenia to Adjustment Reactions

THERE ARE ANOREXICS who are schizophrenic; there are anorexics
who are functioning on a borderline level (and/or who have been
previously diagnosed as schizophrenic, and whose rituals and restric-
tions are serving the function of protecting against a schizophrenic
break. At the other end of the spectrum, there are relatively well-
functioning teenagers who may not have a diagnosis any more severe
than "adolescent adjustment reaction" who get into a brief anorexic
period, and whose over-dieting creates a pathological picture of its
own (with obsessiveness, rituals, lessened capacity for concentration,
withdrawal from social activities, and so on.)

Deborah Brenner, 1984
p. 8

〿

Awareness of the Level of Object Relations Avoids Serious
Treatment Errors

THE BULIMIC [and anorexic] syndromes represent a wide range of
psychopathology. There are bulimics who have predominantly structural conflicts, without significant ego defects; mixed cases where both
structural conflicts and ego defects are present; and further along the
continuum, bulimics who have structural defects and/or developmental arrest in object relations. On the upper end of this continuum,
we can expect to find bulimics who are better oriented to reality, and

whose separation of self and object representations is sufficient to engage in a transference in which the therapist is maintained as a relatively whole displaced object. With these patients interpretation of the transference is possible.

On the other extreme are those bulimics whose failure of differentiation of self from object images leads them to experience the therapist as part of a self object unit, a potential gratifier of unfulfilled needs. If patients' bingeing and vomiting acts as a means of holding together a potentially fragmented self, the therapist doesn't interpret the behavior as a defense against aggressive id impulses and for the present doesn't interfere with the behavior. Awareness of the level of object representations avoids those serious treatment errors that may lead to the patient regressing, decompensating, fleeing treatment, or acting out even more destructively.

Joyce Kraus Aronson, 1986
p. 679

A Continuum of Weight Preoccupation Disorders

OUR DATA SUGGEST a continuum of weight preoccupation disorders, which start subclinically with large numbers of culturally influenced women who are preoccupied with their weight. In this view, as additional psychopathological and/or physiological burdens are superimposed on basic preoccupation with weight, we would expect to see, first, women who develop subdiagnostic eating disorders, then a more severely impaired group with so-called normal-weight bulimia, and then a still more severely ill group who have anorexia nervosa with or without bulimic features.

Joel Yager, John Landsverk, and Carole Edelstein, 1987
p. 1177

A Multidimensional Concept Leads to More Appropriate Comprehensive Treatment

TREATMENT OF an illness should grow rationally from the clinician's understanding and conceptualization of the nature of the illness. It is therefore important to have a comprehensive and scientific understanding of the eating disorders (to the extent this information is available) in order to adequately treat these patients. Narrow concepts of etiology based on the belief that the eating disorders spring solely from a single abnormality of neurochemistry, from a specific abnormal family dynamic, or from a particular preexisting disease such as depressive illness will lead logically but unfortunately to restricted treatments that fail to appreciate the global nature of the disorder. In contrast, a multidimensional concept of origin that appreciates the interactive nature of at least several risk factors will lead to more appropriate comprehensive treatment.

Arnold Andersen, 1990
p. 138

3

Countertransference

Patients' Unacknowledged Emotions May Be Acted Out
by the Therapist

IT IS INTERESTING to note how, in the extremes of countertransference, precisely those emotions of the physician come into play which these patients are incapable of accepting or acknowledging in themselves. Instead of becoming aware of any positive or negative transference, they try to lure the physician into assuming certain roles. The more successful they are in inducing him to pamper or punish them, the more chaotic the situation becomes. For in "counteraction," the analyst now represents those very emotional impulses which the patients have to fend off within themselves.

Helmut Thomä, 1967
p. 309

The Therapist Is Provoked into Counter-Acting Out

ONE PHYSICIAN will try to help with kindness, another will experiment with strict diets, and neither course will be successful. Not surprisingly, the physician soon becomes aware of his own helplessness and of the futility of all his efforts at treating the patient's alarming cachexia. His concern arouses his own defense mechanisms and releases all kinds of countertransference attitudes. The patient's acting out provokes the physician into counter-acting out, be it with indulgence or punishment.

Helmut Thomä, 1967
p. 450

己

Our Boredom Should Alert Us to the Patient's Narcissistic Defense against Affects

OUR BOREDOM AND sleepiness should alert us to the possibility that this is in response to the patient's narcissistic defense against affects. Though the analyst's withdrawal may be defensive, I do not believe that it is necessarily neurotic—it is a very human response to the patient's state of non-relatedness.

Arnold Modell, 1973
p. 275

己

The Cadaverous Appearance Keeps the Therapist Anxious

THE CADAVEROUS appearance arouses strong reactions and thus interferes with all human relationships; it also keeps the therapist anxious and concerned and hinders the progress of treatment.

Hilde Bruch, 1977
p. 107

己

The Capacity of the Therapist to Bear Feelings of Anger, Hopelessness, Manipulation, and Powerlessness Is of the Greatest Importance

PSYCHOTHERAPY WITH anorectic patients leads to intense emotional reactions in the therapist; perhaps the most intense encountered in a therapeutic relationship. However, the capacity of the therapist to bear these feelings of anger, hopelessness, manipulation, and powerlessness is of the greatest importance for the treatment process. It is precisely when the patient can attribute these feelings to a therapist, who can accept and endure these feelings himself, that the patient is first able to achieve personality change and to experience a greater sense of intrapsychic integration.

Bertram J. Cohler, 1977
p. 353

The Therapist May Turn to Behavioral Manipulation out of Despair

TYPICALLY, A therapist is consulted when the patient's physical condition has seriously deteriorated, increasing the risk of fatality. The patient's disturbance, is, of course, reflected in her emaciation. During periods of crisis in psychotherapy, however, weight gained is frequently lost, leading to increased criticism of treatment from both the patient's family and other mental health professionals. Such criticisms tend to make the therapist feel inadequate in providing good treatment, a feeling which is intensified by the patient's challenge that he (the therapist) cannot be of help and that she (the patient) will never get well. Additionally, the therapist is often faced with the prospect of treating a patient who does not believe that she is ill and who is terrified of the possibility that her therapist might control food intake and, therefore, her life. Considering the intensity of anger and despair evoked in the therapist by prolonged psychotherapeutic contact with anorectic patients, it is little wonder that those who find themselves in the position of having to treat such patients often have recourse to behavioral manipulation and modification.

Bertram J. Cohler, 1977
p. 353

己

The Patients Create Despair

THESE PATIENTS bring material to analysis in a very particular way, for example, they may speak in a way which seems calculated to communicate or create despair and a sense of hopelessness in themselves and in the analyst, although apparently wanting understanding.

Betty Joseph, 1982
p. 449

己

Some Therapists May Be Ill-Suited for Work with Adolescent Anorexics

THE THERAPIST must be able to keep in check any impulse to blame or scold—to see the patient as stubborn, spoiled, or manipulative—or to act precipitously to alleviate the patient's suffering with promises or quick remedies. He or she must also be intuitive, and must know how to monitor and pace interventions—when to probe gently and when to hold back and wait patiently. Above all, the therapist must evidence genuine spontaneity and humor, along with a flair for the dramatic—characteristics deeply felt and shared by adolescents generally, and needing to be evoked in the anorexic. Thus, the therapists who tend toward strict neutrality and distance, who are rigid, who are put off by challenges and provocation, or who require some tangible evidence of the fruits of their labor may be ill-suited for work with this population, and are well advised to avoid it.

Michael Strober and Joel Yager, 1984
p. 375

己

Disconfirming the Patient's Belief in the Destructiveness of Self-Assertion

THE PATIENT attempts, in the relative safety of the therapeutic situation, to try out a range of oppositional, aggressive behavior, taking the risk that the therapist will know how to handle it and will not be as upset by it as her parents would be. The extreme nature of her assertiveness results in part because of its newness and a long overdue self-indulgence and abandon, and in part out of guilt; in other words, assertiveness is expressed in extreme ways in a manner which invites disapproval and punishment. The patient unconsciously observes the therapist's reaction. If the therapist is not upset by such behavior, he will help to disconfirm the patient's belief in the destructiveness of self-assertive, non-compliant behavior and diminish her separation guilt.

Michael Friedman, 1985
p. 36

己

Some Therapists Approach Anorexics Critically and with Open Dislike

I FEEL THAT some of the treatment difficulties are related to the therapist's often unexamined suspicion that the patient's denial of illness indicates dishonesty. Therapists tend to deal with this dishonesty as if patients could change it through an act of will. For this reason, some therapists approach and evaluate anorexic patients in a critical manner, with a certain guardedness and prejudice, or even with open dislike.

Hilde Bruch, 1988
p. 11

⊐

The Therapist May Feel Needy and Greedy

IN SPITE OF HER regular attendance, for many months the feeling in the sessions was one of a lack of involvement and "inner absence." I believe she achieved this by projecting into me what she could not permit herself to feel. I found myself feeling that I was the needy greedy person who wanted to give her something to satisfy myself. At times I caught myself wanting to reach and comfort her and I feared her loss. Certainly she did not wish to *need* my analytic food.

Marjorie P. Sprince, 1988
p. 77

⊐

The Therapist May Feel Rendered Invisible

AS THERAPISTS, we try to occupy the always hard won role of "the other person" for the anorexic patient and to be adequate to the task and risks involved in taking on the role. But then it may be only to find that many a patient is trapped in the straitjacket of what she has worked at so unremittingly and succeeded at all too well, viz., the pathological self-sufficiency defensive organization carried to the ascetic extreme. In this pathologically or pseudo-autonomous position and inclined to polarized, heaven-or-hell extremes in thinking, the anorexic patient is obliged to destroy or refuse much that is offered, giving rise to potential countertransference matters which can severely test all the resources of the empathic holding environment. The therapist, or whoever constitutes "the other," must be able to retain within his own periodically very distressed and aggression-laded self some cohesive and differentiated idea or belief that psychotherapeutic work can indeed be potentially gratifying and eventually will be the human nutriment which will play a positive part in the patient's later integration. Otherwise, the therapist feels repulsed and held under arrest by the sadly accusing patient or, even harder to tolerate, rendered invisible and, in a sense, dead or "missing in action."

R. Ian Story, 1990
p. 5

⊒

Countertransference with the Borderline Eating-disordered Patient

THE THERAPIST should be aware of the countertransference issues that arise when treating the borderline patient. These patients do not just tell the therapist how they feel; they make the therapist feel it! This may result in anger, defensiveness, helplessness, guilt, and even retaliation on the part of the therapist.

Amy Baker Dennis and Randy Sansone, 1991
p. 141

⊒

Unrealistic "Tests of Caring" Can Cripple the Most Conscientious of Therapists

SOME THERAPISTS are not comfortable with the intense transference and ever-present demandingness and neediness of borderline patients with eating disorders. These patients require consistency, continuity, and patience. The crisis-to-crisis nature of treatment, together with the patients' repetitive self-destructive behavior and/or unrealistic "tests of caring," can cripple the most conscientious of therapists. We have seen colleagues respond to these pressures through disorganization, chronic fatigue, franticness, guilt, chronic eating, or increased drug and alcohol use. . . . We recommend that any therapist who works with an eating disorder patient with borderline personality disorder should participate in ongoing, regular supervision and should actively confront countertransference reactions. This will help the therapist maintain a more positive attitude toward and a more objective perspective on the patient.

Amy Baker Dennis and Randy Sansone, 1991
p. 142

日

The Therapist May Be Less Spontaneous, Less Relaxed, and More Careful with Interventions

T REATMENT WITH these patients often begins under a cloak of great vigilance, with a readiness to be distrustful. They are, as it were, there, but with one foot out the door. Swiftly, all aspects of the therapist, including attire, tone of voice, or shifting of body, come under careful scrutiny. If the therapist recalls an incident or memory mentioned sessions before, or responds in a particularly empathic manner, then the patient feels "together" and whole and considers the therapist as an ally. However, if the therapist cancels a session or responds with the slightest trace of irritation in his or her voice, then the patient reacts with hurt and pain and regards the therapist as hostile, distant, and uncaring. My own counterreaction with these patients has been one of being viewed under a microscope. Not only is my every movement closely monitored (often incredibly accurately), but my comments are carefully scrutinized, reconnoitered, and regarded as evidence to weigh before allowing the relationship to continue and possibly deepen. This stance evokes a marked countervigilance and hypercaution on my part. Realizing that interpretations will be met with an overreaction and taken as a personal attack, I have found myself at times less spontaneous, less relaxed, and more careful with my interventions.

Howard Lerner, 1991
p. 112

日

The Therapist Is Repeatedly Placed in the Role of the Bad Object

TREATERS WHO work with these patients can easily become frustrated if they fail to understand that they will be repeatedly placed, via projective identification, in the role of the "bad object." The patients will attempt to make others feel as wretched as they themselves sometimes do, while simultaneously attempting to master their traumas by reversal. This major internalized object relations paradigm is a necessary mode of survival for such patients.

Kathryn Zerbe, 1992
p. 179

4

Defending against Affect

Dangerous to Be Aware of One's Own Affect

A STRONG AFFECT that is not overwhelming brings with it an experience of self; it impels integration and synthesis as it impels purposiveness and mastery, working in many ways as does instinctual drive. . . . The experience of passion is pleasurable per se. It affords an internal sense of psychological action and integration, a melding of affect, thought and action that produces the experience of actuality, when it achieves adaptive discharge. Not to feel strongly is to be deprived of self-affirmation and to experience one's self as diffuse, as seen in the late adolescent who has deactivated himself in defense against a too strong affect or impulse, and who then fears that he cannot love and therefore cannot define himself either with regard to object or to work.

Mr. A's process of binding affect was to somaticize it and then to bind the somatic form, in this instance his body form in the literal sense. It was through reduction in body size that he thought he could achieve attachment to others and it was because of his preoccupation with weight loss that he suffered detachment from them. The paradox was the conflict between his pain of separation and his dread of closeness, between his longing for feeling engaged and his desire for independence which for him could only be affective autarchy. To allow himself contact with his own feelings meant violent dissolution.

That body of his was a beast that would devour him or others and that had to be disarmed by being weakened.

Paul Seton, 1972
p. 18

〓

Eating and Vomiting as a Way of Becoming a Feelingless Thing

THIS PATIENT SAID that in the past all she ever wanted to do was to die and to be dead and to stop feeling, and that eating and vomiting, "full and empty," was a way of stopping feelings. She now said that she was experiencing a different kind of sadness than any which she had previously experienced. Sadness now included there being "something to be sad about," a new development for her. She was sad about the memory of her relationship with me and my absence during intervals between sessions. With greater integration and continuity of experience, and "something to be sad about," she felt "human," rather than making herself into a "feelingless thing" which she said she had done in the past. Any disruption of the continuity of our relationship now led to the sadness but she *no longer had the global, all-encompassing pain.* As to causes of disruption, she showed *less* disturbance when I went away for a week than when I cancelled one session or accepted a telephone call or rustled papers during a session. The reason she gave for this difference was that when I went away for a week she became "numb and dead again, and did not know it; time stopped so I didn't really wait for you to return." When I cancelled one session, however, she remained "alive," and had to "stretch" her ability to wait for the next session, and suffered. It was this kind of experience that made her "question whether [she] ever should have come to life."

Alfred Flarsheim, 1975
p. 186

〓

"Deadness" as a Necessary Defense

SHE USED THE term "being dead" to refer to her way of relieving pain and explosive feelings by eating and vomiting. Since all feelings were explosively painful, a state of affective "deadness" was a necessary defense, and suicidal impulses were a logical outcome. She went to a restaurant to eat and then vomit immediately after each session. This symptom was clearly life-saving, serving, as she described it, to achieve "deadness" as a defense against painful awareness of separateness, which she said would require suicide. Later she was able to tell me that the reason it had taken two years for her to tell me about the eating and vomiting was that she had feared that any doctor would try to "cure" such a symptom; and she would perish.

Alfred Flarsheim, 1975
p. 167

Alleviation of Unbearable Affects

BOTH ANOREXIC and bulimic patients use food magically and concretely to control primitive and overwhelming affects associated with separation and loss. Both battle with the pain and terror of an empty void which they are impelled to fill with food. The anorexic avoids the pain of emptiness by denying the empty space and concretely decreasing the void. The bulimic seeks endlessly to fill the space. In both illnesses there is a degree of object constancy with a person who is there and not there at the same time—that is to say, unpredictably appearing and disappearing—a nourishing and not nourishing mother. It is likely that the early process of internalizing affects surrounding such devastating nurturing experiences is a decisive factor in the development of this type of pathology.

Marjorie Sprince, 1984
p. 214

⊒

Fear of Feelings

OF THE MAJOR themes encountered in the treatment of such (anorexic) individuals, fear of, and discomfort with feelings clearly stands out. There is a belief that feelings will cause rejection by significant others and are a burden to these others. One woman thought that when she was depressed or angry or even happy, she would be unacceptable to anyone close to her. She confessed a secret thought that her therapist would terminate treatment if she dared to reveal feelings since this would either offend him or cause her to become a nuisance. She had the impression that therapy was supposed to rid her of troublesome affects.

Jules Bemporad and John Ratey, 1985
p. 458

⊒

As the Patient Begins to Express Feelings in Words There Is Less Need to Act Them Out with Food

MS. Y USED bingeing both to express and to control overwhelming feelings. For example, Ms. Y had become filled with anxiety and sexual excitement after she had resisted the urge to invite a man to whom she had been attracted to her apartment. After she had hastily said goodnight, she rushed out to a fast food restaurant and binged. Likewise, when she had been furious about a brief telephone message from her mother (whom she felt should be more attentive to her) Ms. Y began to eat compulsively. This was similar to her response to the powerful, conflicted feelings about her promotion. As Ms. Y began to express feelings more directly in words, and was able to be aware of distinct and vivid emotions, this use of action to contain and express feelings diminished.

Lynn Whisnant Reiser, 1988
p. 383

〓

Little Affect Tolerance

THE ONGOING psychoanalytic process also led to my patients' discovery that they had very little *affect tolerance* and that this had been
masked not only by the neurotic symptoms but more particularly by
addictive behavior.

Joyce McDougall, 1989
p. 107

〓

Achieving Altered Ego States Can Be an Unconscious
Motive for Bingeing

WHILE BULIMIC patients stress *manifest* components of the binge—the
intake of food and the acts of either vomiting or purging—they
frequently gloss over the change in state of consciousness. Since
bulimic patients do not complain of these aspects of their experience
and often refer to them only indirectly, clinicians have not usually
regarded them as symptoms. In descriptions of how they responded to
the bingeing or purging, patients complain of feeling terrible—guilty,
self-critical, or numb—and report intense dysphoria during and after
bingeing (although, especially early in the course of the disorder,
patients may report pleasure at the beginning of the eating). This
account of dysphoria masks the importance of the "difference" from
how they felt before bingeing. "Relief" is described in terms of relief
from the craving to binge. This further obscures underlying unconscious motivation to defend against conflicting thoughts and affects.

For some bulimic individuals, achieving this change in feeling state
may constitute a powerful primary conscious rather than incidental
aim of bingeing. Life conflicts that evoke strong affective arousal—for
example, lust, anger, competitive aggression, loneliness—frequently

precede and precipitate binges. Achieving altered ego states can be an unconscious motive for bingeing.

Lynn Whisnant Reiser, 1990
p. 245

⊒

Dissociative Abilities of the Borderline Bulimic

I HAVE FOUND that many eating-disordered patients will report a history of dissociative abilities, particularly those, of course, who are in the "borderline" range of psychopathology and/or who have experienced the trauma of physical or sexual abuse. In fact, several of my bulimic patients have reported being "better" at dissociating spontaneously as children than they are now. One patient described how as a child she used to be able to "go numb" at will to find relief from her emotional pain, and how as she got older she began to lose this ability. During one session, she realized with a jolt that she was now using her bulimia and her drug use as external techniques to reach the same dissociative state she had been able to reach internally as a child.

Susan Sands, 1991
p. 40

⊒

Silence May Be a Consequence of Suppression of Intense Feelings

IN MY EXPERIENCE and that of colleagues, it has not been found that the weight loss interferes with thinking or the ability to utilize analytic treatment. . . . Long periods of silence were not reflective of a problem in thinking or an absence of feeling: quite the reverse. The silence was a consequence of such frightening thoughts and intense feelings that the patient felt overwhelmed by them and so felt it necessary to suppress them by all means possible, including silence. It may be that in some cases when a patient is silent and is asked by the therapist what is on her mind, the reply may be "nothing." This less than candid response and defensive attempt at minimizing anxiety could well be misconstrued as the patient's having nothing on her mind.

Ira Mintz, 1992b
p. 188

5

Developmental Issues

Separation and Individuation Are Interfered with in All Phases of the Child's Development

THESE PATIENTS have been attached to a domineering and controlling mother who attempts to attain passive submission and perfection for the child as her own fulfillment. Power and control exerted by the omnipotent mother is overwhelming, remarkably interfering with separation and individuation in all phases of the child's development.

John Sours, 1974
p. 571

Abstract Thinking and Independent Evaluation Are Deficient

WE HAVE LEARNED from Piaget that the capacity to think, conceptual development, goes through definite stages. Though the potential for this step-by-step development is inherent in the human endowment, for appropriate maturation it needs an encouraging environment. It seems that in anorexic youngsters such encouragement is insufficient. They continue to function with the moral convictions and style of thinking of early childhood. Piaget called this the phase of preconceptual or concrete operations; it is also called the period of egocentricity and is characterized by concepts of magical effectiveness. Anorexics seem to be stuck in this phase, at least in the way they approach personal problems, and the development of the characteristic adolescent phase that involves the capacity for formal operations with the ability for abstract thinking and independent evaluation is deficient in them, or even completely absent.

Hilde Bruch, 1978
p. 48

弓

The Mirroring Phase

T HE BEGINNING of the disturbance appears to be located at the level of the "mirroring phase" within which the mother is unable to see and reflect the child as itself. A specific conflict emerges in the child's sense of self, between the body as a visible aspect of itself, and its feeling "unseen" by the parent. The loss of body weight is a desperate appeal to the parents to make psychic contact with the "unseen" person.

Ana-Maria Rizzuto, Ross K. Peterson, and Marilyn Reed, 1981
p. 471

弓

Pathological Union of the Child's Special Needs with the Parents' Special Sensitivity

I DENTIFICATION without mirroring translates developmentally into a split off sense of specialness combined with an excessive compliance, a collusive bond between mother and child which is reminiscent of what Greenacre calls a focal symbiosis, a relationship in which there is a "pathological union of the child's special needs with the parents' special sensitivity." Within this collusive bond, compliance fosters subordination of the' child's self to the subservient position of a narcissistic extension of the mother. The daughter perceives her mother as experiencing increasing difficulties mirroring any thoughts, feelings, or actions which differ from the mother's; and *pari passu* we see mothers, whose daughters have anorexia who increasingly need their daughters as a narcissistic extension of themselves in order to feel whole and alive.

Richard Geist, 1984
p. 9

己

A Paucity of Self-Regulating Structure

I WOULD SUGGEST that the reason anorexic girls retreat from all pleasure involves the disparity between tantalizing satisfactions and a paucity of self-regulating structure capable of containing their appetites, for all those beatific and sensuous pleasures enjoyed by peers feel uncontrollable. As one patient suggested, "To enjoy myself would be like flying around a Maypole; I'd be terrified that I would eventually fly off into space." Thus the anorexic patient is not anchored in herself, but feels rigidly controlled by an intrusive environment.

Richard Geist, 1985
p. 277

己

Failure of Splitting

THE INFANT MUST be able to split in order to feed safely without the intrusion of the anxiety that he is harming his mother, and without the anxiety that she will harm him. It is necessary for an infant to feel that the mother who is taking care of him is fully loving and has no connection whatever with the mother who "hurts" him by making him wait. The anxiety arising from the thought that the nurturing mother and the frustrating mother are one and the same would rob the infant of the security that he needs in order to feed safely. . . .

The following clinical material is taken from an intensive psycho-therapy of an 18-year-old woman with anorexia nervosa.

Over a period of almost a year, Ms. S starved herself almost to death because her mother's food (which she generalized to include all food) was "too rich." This patient professed deep love for her mother and was unable to think of a single thing about her mother that she did not like and admire. Not only was her mother's food too rich, it was also at times felt to be "too good to eat"; in fact, the patient did not even like to see her mother's food being cooked because it was too good to cook. Eventually, in the course of therapy, one of the patient's central underlying conflicts was clarified: her mother was "too good to hate." (This was not a matter of failure of repression in relation to an ambivalently loved mother; this patient was unable to utilize effectively even the more primitive defense of splitting in relation to a mother experienced as a collection of part-objects.)

Thomas Ogden, 1986
pp. 54, 56

ㄹ

Attempting to Make Food a Reliable Transitional Object to Undo the Mother's Unreliability

Bulimics, by their use and abuse of food, are attempting to make of food a reliable transitional object, as a way to undo the mother's frightening unreliability. Two features of transitional objects are important to this contention: (1) the transitional object provides the sensory experience of the mother, that is, warmth, softness, and smell; and (2) it is a sensory experience the person can provide for herself whenever she needs it.

Camay Woodall, 1987
p. 183

ㄹ

Women are Prone to Eating Disorders because of the Developmental Hazards of Their Psychosexual Development

W HEN THE MOTHER-DAUGHTER relationship is overly close and hostile–dependent, when the mother unconsciously refuses to let go and the daughter is unable to achieve actual or psychological separation or a distinct identity of her own, then the stage is set for many types of psychopathology. Depression and eating disorders are among the most common of these, and often go together.

This is not to assert that such developmental factors are in themselves sufficient to explain the onset of an eating disorder in a given individual. All psychopathology is multidetermined, and other specific features of the family constellation and the individual's personal history obviously must play a role. Nor is it simplistically implied that mothers are in some sense "to blame" for their daughters' failures in separation and individuation. Rather, understanding the peculiar hazards of the psychosexual developmental process for mothers and daughters alike can throw light on why women are so much more prone than men to develop eating disorders, usually at critical stages of separation from mother and family.

Hilary J. Beattie, 1988
p. 456

Struggling to Create an External, Concrete, and Specific Transitional Object

T HESE INDIVIDUALS, because of their concrete, nonsymbolic mode of operation, are not able to move to an external non-bodily transitional object. They seem instead to struggle to *create* a transitional object which *is* external, concrete, and specific. This transitional object becomes food, and it is temporarily able to regulate affective states. The effectiveness of the object is fleeting, however, and can remain no more fixed in emotional consciousness than the defective internal images of body, self, or other. Food is the first transitional object—the bridge between mother and infant. It is not the mother, but it represents her, and is an extension of her body. Food is, however, more a symbolic equation than a true symbol. These psychological deficits are most profoundly elaborated in bulimia. The pathological developmental course which leaves the young individual with a defective or absent body image, a defective sense of wholeness, and impaired function is the preverbal bedrock of missed experience that appropriate therapeutic efforts must address.

David Krueger, 1988
p. 61

己

"No" Says "I Am Not an Extension of You"

THE FIRST WORDS used are metaphors for the body, and its separateness from the mother. The infant who learns to say "no" states a distinctness from the parent. "No" says "I am not an extension of you. I am me, and I am in charge of me." This is also the attempt of the anorexic who says "no" to food proffered by her parents: "I don't need you or anything you give me."

David Krueger, 1988
p. 67

己

Unable to Defend Legitimate Self-Interest, the Patient May Regress to Earlier Stages of Orality

FEELING OUT OF control . . . and unable to use her mouth effectively to verbalize, define, and defend her legitimate self-interest, she regresses back to earlier stages of orality. This early feeding stage contains elements of drive satisfaction and frustration, and ego satisfaction and frustration. From the point of drive satisfaction, sucking and eating provide the earliest form of inner warmth, nourishment, and security. Early aggressive drives are also satisfied by sucking and biting. Viewed from the developing ego, satisfaction occurs through the early sense of mastery, by sucking and eating. Restless activity associated with signs of hunger is rewarded by the sensitive, nourishing mother by feeding with relief of tension.

Ira Mintz, 1988
p. 162

Deficient in Modulating and Containing Emotion

T HE UNAVAILABILITY of her mother in early childhood may have left Ms. Y deficient in modulating and containing emotion. Ms. Y was not bulimic except during times when she felt under particular stress. She then turned to a familiar but unsatisfactory way of comfort. Ms. Y managed any strong feelings – anger, sexuality, despair, or triumph – by bingeing. For Ms. Y, the binge represented both a symptom of distress and an attempt to deal with painful feelings.

Lynn Whisnant Reiser, 1988
p. 390

Conflict with Mother Inhibits the Development of the Communicative Functions of Language

V ERBAL LANGUAGE which has acquired full richness for affective contact has the power to affect the body ("I feel what you say in the pit of my stomach"), to soothe in inner dialogue ("I hear my mother saying: It is O.K."), to share intersubjective experience ("I understand how you feel"), and to describe the world and psychic reality. This is the positive side of its potential. On the other hand, the partial failure of language to achieve its affective and communicative function, due to disturbances in early patterns of mother–child relatedness, may bring about the conditions for somatic reactions, fear of the power of words, feelings of not being seen and heard and, the disappearance of the wish to communicate. The process is circular: the conflict with the object inhibits the development of the *communicative* functions of language. The child defends against the repetition of the trauma of failed affective contact in preverbal and verbal exchanges because he/she has already experienced the pain of words without affect. As a result the child avoids communication.

Ana-Maria Rizzuto, 1988
p. 376

르

The Developmental Framework of the Separation-Individuation Process Can Clarify the Early Transference Struggles in Therapy

THE INTENSE transference–countertransference engagement, the "pull–push" dance, the scenario of "I feel so helpless, inadequate and alone – you must help me to function – but if you do I will feel hurt and enraged – your help will make me feel more helpless and over-whelmed – you must help me" was repetitive in her behavior and seemed to preoccupy her thinking. As the months passed the analyst began to gain an appreciation and understanding of this seemingly chaotic drama as reflecting derivatives of a developmental lag, and that this could be conceptualized in terms of unresolved conflicts of the rapprochement subphase of the separation-individuation process.

This subphase of the separation-individuation process, spanning the period from about sixteen months to twenty four months of age has been described as the "nexus" of this developmental process and the "mainspring of man's eternal struggle against both fusion and isolation." In the rapprochement subphase the maturation of percep-tual, cognitive and motoric skills has made the junior toddler increas-ingly aware of his separateness from his mother and increasingly aware of his vulnerability, aloneness, smallness and dependency. His devel-opmentally normal sense of shared parental omnipotence as well as fantasies of his own omnipotence, in the dual oneness of the symbiosis are threatened and necessarily deflated. The anger stimulated towards the now separate and relatively less available parent, the object he both loves and now realizes he desperately needs, increases the threat of losing the mother or being lost from her. On the one hand the toddler wants to exercise his newly found autonomy and independence fully; on the other hand, he painfully feels the loss of his former sense of omnipotence and is distressed by his relative helplessness.

Using this developmental framework, the expression in the analysis of Sarah's intrapsychic conflicts took on clearer definition and the enacted intense, frantic, stagnating, circular quality of her interpersonal struggles, vividly reflected in the transference, took on greater meaning.

Newell Fischer, 1989
p. 45

◫

For Women, to Increase or Lose Weight at Any Life Stage Can Reactivate Separation-Individuation Conflicts that Have No Parallel for Men

THE WOMAN HAS three prototypic, normal psychophysiological experiences in her life in which her body contour is altered significantly: puberty, pregnancy, and before and after menstrual periods. In puberty, there is an increase in adipose tissue in the breasts, thighs, and hips; in pregnancy, there is an obvious body-size increase; and before and after the menses, there is a weight increase and subsequent loss.

These phases are associated with various stages of separation-individuation. For example, at puberty, conflict in the female might be around whether to remain mother's preoedipal girl or to become a genitally sexual adolescent with a more autonomous self. At pregnancy, or at each menstrual period, a struggle may arise over unconsciously remaining mother's child (i.e., by identifying with the fetus or by not accepting the nurturing role), or becoming a more mature sexual woman substituting a real child of her own for the child imago.

Hence, to increase or lose weight at any life stage can reactivate separation-individuation issues for the woman in a way with which the man has no parallel. For although his body changes in puberty and at other life stages, its basic form is not altered as radically as the woman's.

Laura Arens Fuerstein, 1989
p. 169

Food Is More Trustworthy because It's Always There

THE PERSON WHO has an eating disorder has "given up" on receiving empathic attunement from the caregiving surround and has turned instead to a nonhuman (and thus more reliable) substitute to find the comfort and inspiration she seeks. As one of my patients put it, "There was no one who I could trust to share the deep pain. Food was more trustworthy, because food was always there." Food, of course, is a particularly compelling substitute since it is the first bridge between self and selfobject—the first medium for the transmission of soothing and comfort.

Susan Sands, 1989
p. 87

The Therapist Must Understand the Importance of the Symptoms in Maintaining Self-Esteem and Self-Cohesion

EATING DISORDERS are complex and require the therapist's patience and willingness to explore many possible dynamics before they even begin to respond to therapy. Understanding the importance of the symptoms in the maintenance of self-esteem and self-cohesion can help the therapist to have patience with stubborn, recalcitrant symptoms and to understand why simply making unconscious fears and fantasies conscious is not enough to lead to change.

Diane Barth, 1991
p. 227

己

The Greater the Impairment of the Sense of Separation of Self from Object, the More Severe Are the Symptoms

ANOREXIA NERVOSA is an expression of defective ego development arising from varying degrees of failure to resolve the separation-individuation processes and of failure to develop a sense of individuality. This determines the character of disturbances in object relationships. The more serious the symptoms of the illness, the more intense or primitive is the symbiotic level of functioning; although mild symptoms do not necessarily mean the opposite. Stating this in the reverse, the greater the impairment of the sense of separation of self from object, the more severe are the symptoms likely to be. This can be said of all psychosomatic illnesses, but it can be seen in very blatant form in anorexia nervosa.

Cecil Mushatt, 1992
p. 302

己

Emphasis Should Be on the Early Ego-defective Development

PRIMARY EMPHASIS on sexual conflicts, especially oedipal, as causative psychological factors in anorexia nervosa is a limiting approach to the problem. The symptomatology and sexual and aggressive conflicts and fantasies, with the accompanying defenses, can best be understood within the framework of the process of separation of self from object and the seemingly insoluble dilemma in regard to the struggle to achieve a sense of separateness and individuality. This has its effects on the development of the body image, with its internalized symbolic representations of the environment, and through the body image on the ego, superego, and instinctual life. Anorexia nervosa is an expression of ego-defective development arising from varying degrees of failure to resolve the process of developing a sense of individuality.

Cecil Mushatt, 1992
p. 308

6

Dynamics

Early Disappointments Lead to Permanent Distrust

ALL THE BITTERNESS and pain which related to the earliest disappointments by mother, and which were primarily bound up with feeding, care, affection, remained the source of her permanent distrust of everybody.

Sandor Lorand, 1943
p. 290

Their Aesthetic and Narcissistic Pretensions Hide an Authentic Hunger for Life

THEY ACT AS IF they were not hungry, they reject maturity and sexuality, and disparage their feminine and erotic strivings. But their real hunger for love and thirst for life are betrayed by the importance they attach to food in their drawings and dreams, in the way they gulp down scraps from the refrigerator, and in their need to know that food is amply available.

H. Hiltmann and G. Clauser, 1961
p. 168

51

No Pleasure without Remorse

For a psychodynamic understanding it is essential to note that these patients experience no real satisfaction, no pleasure, without remorse or guilt feelings. Everything has to be reversed. The bites taken must be spit out.

Helmut Thomä, 1967
p. 441

Dependency of the Inside on Something Outside Brings About an Unbearable Conflict

Both in fact and in subjective experience, the biological act of taking in, of incorporation, is a prototype of object finding, of making contact, and of assimilating an outside thing onto oneself. In the subjective experience of hunger, the ego depends on nature in a twofold way: the need which is to be satisfied comes from the inside, whilst the satisfaction of the drive is provided by an object, which in early life is supplied by another person, usually the mother. This dependency of the inside on something outside brings about an unbearable conflict in anorectic patients and explains why they do not acknowledge any needs or bodily desires.

Helmut Thomä, 1967
p. 441

Food Intake and Body Size Are Manipulated in Both Anorexia and Obesity

Although anorexia and obesity look like extreme opposites, they have many features in common. In both conditions food intake and body size are manipulated in a futile effort to solve or camouflage inner stress or adjustment difficulties. These youngsters do not feel identified with their bodies, but look upon it as an external object over which they must exercise rigid control, as in anorexia, or in relation to which they feel helpless, as lacking in will power, and the result is obesity.

Hilde Bruch, 1977
p. 102

Starvation Itself Has a Distorting Effect

THE STATE OF starvation itself has such a distorting effect on all psychic functioning that no true picture of the psychological problems can be formulated until the worst malnutrition is corrected.

Hilde Bruch, 1977
p. 105

Control over the Body Becomes a Supreme Accomplishment

WHEN YOU ARE SO unhappy and you don't know how to accomplish anything, then to have control over your body becomes a supreme accomplishment. You make out of your body your very own kingdom where you are the tyrant, the absolute dictator.

Hilde Bruch, 1978
p. 65

The Illness Is a Desperate Fight against
Feeling Enslaved

THE VERY FEATURES that are so glowingly described as evidence of superior behavior, are indications of serious maldevelopment. The illness appears to be a desperate fight against feeling enslaved, not permitted or competent to lead a life of their own. This effort, instead of solving only reinforces their difficulties. Changing the body size cannot provide what they need and cannot correct the deficits in their overall development.

Hilde Bruch, 1980
p. 255

≡

Depression May Be a Positive Force

DEPRESSION, MEANING the experience and recognition of hopelessness and despair together with a new sense of loneliness, can, at least at times, be a positive force—reflecting reality and recognition of the actual changes that still need to occur. In the author's view "disease" of many kinds is sometimes an alternative and more primitive (i.e. unrealistic and avoidance-based) response. To experience depression and cope with it may be the price of recovery for the anorectic.

Arthur Crisp, 1980
p. 140

≡

Control of One's Own Body Assures Unconscious
Superiority and Power

IN ANOREXIA NERVOSA, the efforts to magically control one's own body (fantasied as a potentially dangerous enemy) coincide with the unconscious reprojection of that power struggle onto the surrounding environment. The patient's control over her own life and death assures her unconscious superiority and power over all those who try to control her—particularly those who are concerned for her survival.

Otto F. Kernberg, 1980
p. x

〓

Eating, the Earliest Gratifying and Frustrating Experience, Can Be Used for the Expression of Many Conflicts

B Y VIRTUE OF ITS connection with the earliest gratifying and frustrating experiences with the object, eating has the longest and most complex history as a modality for the expression of wishes, aims, and conflicts relating to the object. Eating can be used for the expression of conflicts over loving and being loved, loving and hating, attacking and being attacked, punishing and being punished.

Samuel Ritvo, 1980
p. 453

〓

The Illusion of Supreme Glory

A NOREXIA NERVOSA represents the oxymoronic ultimate in achievement, a conquest of the body by the self whereby the self achieves the illusion of supreme glory. This is an existence which, to the anorectic, has a special reality, even though it is isolating and self-absorbing. This is not the seeking of an adolescent identity, new role choices in the Ericksonian sense. Existence is not taken for granted. Instead, the anorectic is seeking a confirmation that she is alive, whole, and rooted in the present time.

John Sours, 1980
p. 5

Narcissism Masquerades as Puritanism

T HE ANORECTIC struggles against feeling enslaved, manipulated, and exploited. She believes that she has not been given a life of her own. She wants to establish a survival system. Her goal is power, expressed by a grand gesture which gets its energy from the fact that it is difficult to stop anyone from starving herself. She wants to avoid any kind of accommodation to the demands of others, contrary to the compliant, sweet, posture she maintained in her earlier childhood. She treats her body as though it were a threatening entity which, like a demon, needs to be controlled at all times. As her flesh falls away, her soul is revealed, made free again, given shape and nourished by a diet of primitive anger thinly disguised by a falsely appealing, chic narcissism masquerading as Puritanism.

John Sours, 1980
p. 287

A Masochistic Delight in Suffering

T HE CONCEPTUAL and perceptual attainment of absolute power and control of the body, self, parents, and other significant object relations is central to the syndrome. Thus, conceptual and perceptual discrimination is compromised through denial and suppression of individuative feelings and actions. The narcissistic pleasure of attaining supreme thinness obscures, for the anorectic, both the realistic ugliness of cachexia and the painful craving for food. Control of pleasure dissociates body and affective feelings from perceptual impressions and mental representations. The pleasure of limitless energy and hyperactivity nullifies a sense of ineffectiveness, denies fatigue and attenuates both aggressive and libidinal excitement. The pleasure of perfect performance and perfect ego-ideal challenges the exalted ego-ideal of the parents. To prevent a further narcissistic challenge to the parents, which might bring about a painful crisis of conscience for the patient, the anorectic takes a masochistic delight in suffering, which modifies the strain of her archaic, primitive superego.

John Sours, 1980
p. 353

It Is Hard to Abandon Such Terrible Delights for the Uncertain Pleasures of Real Relationships

I GET THE IMPRESSION from the difficulty these patients experience in waiting and being aware of gaps and aware of even the simplest type of guilt that such potentially depressive experiences have been felt by them in infancy, as terrible pain that goes over into torment, and that they have tried to obviate this by taking over the torment, the inflicting of mental pain on to themselves and building it into a world of perverse excitement, and this necessarily militates against any real progress towards the depressive position. It is very hard for our patients to find it possible to abandon such terrible delights for the uncertain pleasures of real relationships.

Betty Joseph, 1982
p. 455

Fear of Being Fat

EMPHASIS ON THE fear of being fat rather than on the reluctance to eat and the desire to be thin in patients with anorexia and in normal women is very significant. This may seem at first sight a relatively unimportant distinction, but it is very valuable for the orientation that it induces towards the patient. It helps to focus on some of the major sources of conflict in anorexics, namely the fear of their voraciousness and insatiability and with this of the intensity of their narcissism; with these are the patient's fear of destructiveness associated with such fantasies and the intolerance of the resulting archaic guilt that bedevils the lives of anorexic patients.

Cecil Mushatt, 1982b
p. 258

⊐

Expectations of Perfection and Omnipotence

IN THE MORE severe cases, it is easy to recognize the expectations of perfection, omnipotence and omniscience, the desire for complete subservience of the mother and the world—i.e., complete control over key persons, internally represented by desire for control over the self and one's body, and the demand to be the one and only, worshipped by all.

Cecil Mushatt, 1982b
p. 264

⊐

A Deficiency of Self-Regulation

THE PATIENT WHO suffers from bulimia or anorexia relates to her body strangely. Sensations of hunger are often suppressed or ignored. At the same time sensations of hunger, fullness, and other sensations in general seem very important. A patient tells me she must go from extreme hunger to extreme fullness and that she cannot tolerate any in-between state. Thus when she gives in to her hunger, she cannot stop after she is satisfied, but she must eat until she is painfully stuffed. One aspect of this is of course the terribly deficient capacity to self-regulate that these patients are burdened with.

Alan Goodsitt, 1983
p. 53

⊐

Intensity of Stimulation Is the Goal

ANOTHER ASPECT of this strange behavior where the patient swings wildly from one extreme state to another may be understood in terms of seeking stimulation. Satisfaction of hunger does not suffice. It is the extreme sensations of hunger and fullness which are sought. Intensity of stimulation is a goal. In this light, we should reexamine the meaning of such typical activities long seen in the eating-disordered patient. I am referring to the hyperactivity—pacing, running, swimming long distances, exercising, and in general being unable to sit in place and simply be with oneself. This manic-like activity is not simply to lose weight, but to experience oneself intensely. I submit that the nature of this activity is self-stimulatory.

Alan Goodsitt, 1983
p. 54

Not Eating Is All the Anorexic Has

WITH THE ONSET of the anorexic syndrome, a subtle but intensely powerful defiance becomes increasingly evident in the patient's stubborn refusal to eat. The decision to starve is maintained in spite of very strong parental pressures and threats. A battle ensues over who is to eat what, and when. The battle expands into all areas of food and eating. What the child is not able to accomplish by open defiance and self-assertion in other areas of her life, she achieves in the very circumscribed area of food. As one patient commented, "Not eating is all I've got."

Ira Mintz, 1983c
p. 88

The Starvation Is a Coalescence of Powerful Forces

PARENTS, FRIENDS, and often physicians continue to suggest, encourage, and coerce anorexic patients to eat, often without recognizing that the starvation represents the coalescence of a series of powerful forces arising from conflicts in childhood, swollen by the multitudinous cares of adolescence, and overdetermined by ambivalence surrounding aggression, sexuality, dependency, and regressed infantile yearnings.

Ira Mintz, 1983d
p. 217

⊐

She Is Trying to Cure Herself of Wanting

THE ANOREXIC is trying to cure herself of wanting, more precisely of being found wanting. Since her wants are much too intense to submit securely to repression, she distills the whole spectrum and dimensionality of them into the narrow range of occupations with intake and body image. But even that is not enough. It works intrapsychically by focusing and riveting her own attention to her fixation and obsession and rituals. But there is always the danger that someone may prove desirable—and lead her into the longing, libido and loneliness she hates and is trying to obliterate. So she secures her intrapsychic procedures with the use of projection. If anyone is to want anything of anyone, it is the other who is to want something of her.

Harold Boris, 1984a
p. 435

⊐

Totally Self-Possessed

NEVER TO BE FOUND wanting, that is her interface. To be totally self-possessed, that is the self she wishes to provide herself. Analysis to such a person is not a welcome procedure.

Harold Boris, 1984a
p. 441

ⴲ

Lives without a Skin

THERE IS NO transitional space, the not-me, but yet not-other space, that transitional phenomena require. The anorectic lives, as it were without a skin. Others in their incandescent desirability, impact on her with detonating force. And this is the problem.

Harold Boris, 1984a
p. 437

ⴲ

Anorexia Is a Full Time Job

THE CONSTANT state of hunger is so obtrusive as to overshadow any other feelings. And the preoccupation with body size, shape and weight is so obsessive as to crowd out any other preoccupations. At its "best" anorexia is a full time job.

Harold Boris, 1984a
p. 435

ⴲ

The Man with Toothache Cannot Fall in Love

IN ANOREXIA NERVOSA the pain of hunger or, alternatively (in bulimia), of glut recalls Freud's aphorism that the man with toothache cannot fall in love.

Harold Boris, 1984b
p. 321

コ

A Safe, Solitary Release of Aggressive and Sexual Urges

THE BULIMIC IS typically so uncomfortable with her aggressive and sexual urges that more usual modes of release are unavailable to her. By raising her abdominal and psychological tension to the bursting point and then dramatically releasing it, as occurs with vomiting, she does achieve some measure of gratification. Moreover, it is a safe, solitary release not involving another.

William J. Swift and Ronelle Letven, 1984
p. 493

コ

Illusionary, Self-soothing

SUCH ACTIVITIES as seeing, smelling, tasting, and even at times, chewing food are utterly neglected. Since food now symbolizes objects which have defaulted on her, or "dropped" her, the eating pattern appears to be an attempt to control an untrustworthy object by magical introjection; although really wanting to be held and cared for, the bulimic instead fills her belly to the bursting point lest she should once again lose the object or be let down by it. This effort to self-soothe proves to be illusionary. True, the threatening internal empty spaces have now vanished, but they are quickly replaced by an explosive, persecutory fullness near the conclusion of the binge. Shethen despises herself for losing control of her urges and her dependence on untrustworthy objects. Self-induced vomiting quickly follows.

William J. Swift and Ronelle Letven, 1984
p. 494

コ

Fear of Spontaneity

ANOTHER PROMINENT theme encountered in the treatment of posta-norexic patients is fear of freedom. Even when no longer expending all of their time and energy in measuring out portions of food, or amount of exercise, they still require an inordinate degree of external struc-ture. They are remarkably reactive rather than proactive individuals. One patient realized how she skillfully manipulated others to tell her what to do so that she could refuse or reluctantly conform. She could only act in opposition or under coercion, never spontaneously.

Jules Bemporad and John Ratey, 1985
p. 460

The Memories which Give Form to the Anorectic Patient's Life Appear Indelibly Etched in the Tissues of the Body

TO ACCOMPANY an anorectic patient into her cachectic world of scattered memories is an arduous task. For the critical memories encountered as one begins this inward journey are not the usual ones; not those stored in the accessible reaches of the preconscious mind, nor even those hidden in the further purview of the unconscious. Initially, the memories which give form to the anorectic patient's life appear indelibly etched in the tissues of the body; they form a disconnected picture of the self which has become lost, as it were, in the interstices of cellular movement. Instead of using her memories as internal catalysts for the outward pursuit of precious ambitions and ideals, and thus achieving a sense of wholeness and vitality, the anorectic girl remains immured in her school girl skin. Bereft of appetizing pleasures, obsessively preoccupied with food, weight, and body, and inwardly driven to joyless, unrealistic perfection; the therapist initially observes only isolated reminders of an enduring and cohesive self.

Richard Geist, 1985
p. 1

⊐

Provides an Unassailable Identity

SELF-STARVATION gets attention, it brings the family into line, and it makes the starver the one who calls the tune. It allows the starver to escape many of the responsibilities and burdens of growing up. Best of all, this strategy provides the starver with an unassailable identity. People may disagree about one girl's good looks, another's singing voice, or a third's cheerleading style, but nobody can disagree about whether a girl who is five foot three and weighs eighty pounds is *thin*.

Katherine Byrne, 1987
p. xiii

⊐

Food Is the Most Concrete Possible Symbol of the Maternal Object

THROUGH CONTROL of food intake and body shape a woman can act out almost every aspect of the ambivalent struggle with the actual and the internalized mother. It can be a way of both demanding and rejecting nurturance, of denying her own passive-dependent cravings and defying the mother through being in absolute control of her own body, both its appearance and its products. It is also a way of resisting identification with the mother (by avoiding a rounded body shape and effective heterosexual relationships). At the same time it is a means both of appeasing the mother's narcissistic needs and of competing with her, by dieting in order to attain a more "perfect" figure. Binge eating serves a multitude of functions, including the sadistic, destructive control of the needed object, but it also soothes, tranquilizes, and alleviates inner rage and tension, depression and loss. Such giving in to regressive wishes is then negated and punished through purging, which itself can give vent to aggression and provide emotional release.

Hilary J. Beattie, 1988
p. 456

Camouflage of the Underlying Problems

W HILE THESE patients suffer from severe dissatisfaction about themselves and their lives, they transfer this dissatisfaction to the body. The body is then treated like something foreign that needs to be protected against getting "fat," and this patients do through excessive discipline and overcontrol. Expressions in the deficiency in overall development are manifested by inaccuracy in perception and control of bodily sensations, confusion of emotional states, inaccuracy in language and concept development, and great fear of social disapproval. The relentless pursuit of thinness can be conceived of as an effort to camouflage these underlying problems.

Hilde Bruch, 1988
p. xxx

Not Having a Right to Life

T HE CRUCIAL issue that emerged over and over again in Julie's treatment in many different forms was her underlying, mostly unconscious belief that she did not deserve to live. The message she had gotten from her parents was that her birth was a horrible mistake that had brought unending misery and shame on the family. She unconsciously believed she had irrevocably spoiled a state of family harmony and peace that she imagined existed before her birth. Her states of deep depression, her belief that she could not have any pleasure in her life, her feeling that she was some sort of nonhuman worm who could survive only by keeping herself isolated and hidden from human society, her conviction that her baby would be contaminated by her presence and would do best by having as little exposure to her as possible, all were derivatives of her core belief that she did not have a right to live. From this core dynamic the symptoms of anorexia nervosa emerge as an understandable solution.

Harriet Goldman, 1988
p. 564

〓

Starving Is an Attack against the Self

INCREASED STARVING reflects an attack against the self and the internalized hated introject. In the process, from the aspect of the ego, the starving patient who cannot be stopped makes the parents and physician feel as helpless and as impotent in their current inability to control her as she has long felt in her inability to control aspects of her relationship with them. The starving is a reflection of a repetition compulsion in which the patient unconsciously identifies with what she perceives is the aggressor, while taking the self as the object of that aggression.

Ira Mintz, 1988
p. 131

〓

I Won't Let You Touch Me with Your Words

THE BULIMAREXIC seems to say all the time: I won't let you touch me with your words. You won't get me to reveal myself to you. I have no intention of hearing you. You don't care to hear me either.

Ana-Maria Rizzuto, 1988
p. 373

〓

To Have No Needs Is to Be All-Powerful

To CHALLENGE death by starvation or suicide can mean to the patient that they are all-powerful and have no needs. They can at least achieve a separateness and an identity. Over the last four years I have been struck by the almost religious fervor in the anorexic's need to develop a body so strong and self-sufficient that it can do without nurture. When one considers that food and touch (also sight and smell) are initially so closely related to the supplying object, it becomes meaningful that food, and often touch, must be denuded of value. Gradually all apparent interest in food and body contact may be removed in favor of the need to achieve the *lack of need*. But this solution can be seen to require further reinforcement when the patient is impelled to prove to herself that not only has she no needs but it is the others who are "needy." Thus she projects her needs onto those around her who experience an impulsion to feed, protect, and nurture *her*.

Marjorie P. Sprince, 1988
p. 75

二

Feel They Must Be Perfect and Compliant to Be Loved so They Retreat from the World

ANOREXIA NERVOSA is a defensive retreat from the world of the living, which is viewed and experienced as exploitative, unempathic, dangerous, and untrustworthy. They do not experience being truly loved for themselves, and instead of withstanding the expectable bruises and failures in healthy intimate relationships, feel they must be beautiful, perfect, and compliant to be loved. Indeed, they feel ugly — intolerant of their inner hurt, envy, rage, and primitive guilt, ensconced in a world of people who do not understand.

Eugene V. Beresin, Christopher Gordon, and
David B. Herzog, 1989
p. 104

ᗼ

We Must Maintain Our Respect for the Complexity of the Unconscious

A SYMPTOM, THEN, is a clue to multiple contexts of communicated meaning. It reveals and conceals simultaneously. Our task is to explore hidden meanings while balancing the multiplicity of their implied contexts. This task requires a willingness to appreciate the symptom despite being unable to restrict the play of its meanings. We must maintain our respect for the complexity of the unconscious.

Paul Hamburg, 1989
p. 134

ᗼ

A Disorder of Recognition of Desire

IN THE COURSE OF my work with patients suffering from eating disorders, it has made increasing sense to me to think of many of these patients as suffering from a disorder of recognition of desire. An important aspect of the experience of these patients is an unconscious fear that the patient does not know what he desires. This leads him to ward off the panic associated with such awareness by behaving as if it is food that is desired. The patient may then obsessionally (usually ritualistically) eat and yet never feel full, since what has been taken in is not a response to a desire for food. Rather, the eating represents an attempt to use food *as if* that is what had been desired when in fact the individual does not know what it is to feel desire.

Thomas Ogden, 1989
p. 243

ᗼ

Psychesoma Dissociation

ANOREXICS EXPERIENCE their self and their body as quite distinct entities, rather than as a psychosomatic unity, and rather than being identified with their body, liking it, enjoying it, caring for it, nurturing and developing it, they hate it and cruelly, unrelentingly attack it. Some feel they can starve the soma to death and yet have the psyche survive, and they are surprised and then enraged when others call that belief delusional and interfere with their efforts to actualize that extreme of psychesoma dissociation.

James Sacksteder, 1989c
p. 38

⊐

Self-Mutilation as an Effort to Avoid Depersonalization

THESE [BULIMIC BORDERLINE] patients often internalize the emotional unavailability of the caretaker as evidence that they are unlovable, worthless, and deserving of punishment. They will then mutilate themselves in an effort to punish themselves, with the body once again becoming a concrete representation of self. Interpersonally, they are repeatedly involved in sadomasochistic relationships. Attachments are marked by clingy neediness that alternates with rageful, paranoid withdrawal. Separation is terrifying because it results in profound emptiness, feelings of abandonment, and ego fragmentation. Self-mutilation often appears not only as an effort to punish the unlovable self, but as an effort to avoid depersonalization.

Craig Johnson, 1991
p. 181

⊐

The Delusion of Omnipotence

IN EVERYDAY LIFE the anorectic is experiencing herself as ineffectual and unable to live up to the expectations of her parents, her teachers, her friends, her therapist. But through her performance as a hunger artist the anorectic achieves immense power.

Louise Kaplan, 1991
p. 465

⊒

A Pervasive Delusion of Omnipotence

ALL MY PATIENTS with subclinical eating disorders have a pervasive delusion of omnipotence that takes the form of an ego defect significantly interfering with reality testing. These patients enter treatment with intense aggressive and libidinal impulses that have clashed with fragile defenses and a deficient superego; this clash produces the delusion that only they are powerful enough to inhibit their own omnipotent impulses, and then only by resorting to masochistic means such as deadening their feelings, starving themselves, recklessly bingeing, provoking attack or repeatedly putting themselves in dangerous situations, or even attempting to kill themselves.

Howard Lerner, 1991
p. 115

⊒

Many Bulimic Patients Have Dissociated Self-states

THAT MANY BULIMIC patients are expert at dissociation is well-known to clinicians; in fact, there is research evidence in support of the dissociative abilities of bulimics. Many portray their bingeing episodes as one might describe a trance state, drug trip, or delirium. Most become wholly identified with—"taken over" by—the bulimic self-state. No amount of cognitive persuasion or exhortation can stop them, because the bulimic self has been dissociated from the more reflective, observing self. The early needs *must* be expressed. To try to talk the bulimic self out of bingeing or purging is like telling a cat stalking a bird to stop its carnivorous pursuit.

Susan Sands, 1991
p. 40

Eating Disorders Involve Both Preoedipal and Oedipal Issues

I ALSO WANT TO emphasize the multilayering of psychopathology, in which issues related to both preoedipal and oedipal development (i.e., deficit and conflict) are intricately interwoven. While I agree with Bruch and Johnson and Connors, among others, that failures in the phase of separation-individuation (roughly 12–36 months of age) are pre-eminent in the genesis of both anorexia nervosa and bulimia nervosa, this does not mean that conflictually based oedipal material is nonexistent or unimportant. The fact that the patient has deficits in the ego system and self-system due to failures in the preoedipal period does not indicate that the patient is preconflictual or that oedipal themes are superfluous. Of course, the opposite is equally true: the fact that an individual is torn about instinctive wishes and urges does not lead to the automatic conclusion that the person is deficit-free in the realms of ego and self. Human psychology is simply too rich and too complex to be encompassed by unidimensional statements.

William James Swift, 1991
p. 55

I Stuff Myself to Be a Mother to Myself

THE SYMBOLIC equation of food and human objects is seen in its simplest form in an adult female patient's remark when examining her episodes of excessive eating: "I need a mother to take care of me, so I stuff myself with food, to be a mother to myself. I'd like you to take me in your arms, and let's pretend I am a baby and you are my mother."

Cecil Mushatt, 1992
p. 305

7

Eating Disorders in Adolescents

Precipitated by a Chain of Pathological Developments

AT AGE TWELVE, Paula started a rigid diet which later developed into anorexia nervosa, following a remark of her father's which concerned her weight and her preference for fattening foods. She had interpreted this remark as a rejection of her developing femininity. Of course, this is only one factor in a chain of pathological developments and traumatic experiences which help to precipitate the manifest symptoms of anorexia nervosa in these girls. In the case of the patient just mentioned, it was found that she had correctly interpreted her father's remark. He had a decided preference for slim, boyish-looking women but even more importantly, as long as she was bodily still infantile, he could be close to her without guilt. I want to emphasize, though, that this was only one contributing factor among many which precipitated her anorexia nervosa.

Melitta Sperling, 1955
p. 148

Mother's Anxiety Increases as the Daughter Approaches Adolescence

A NOT RARE occurrence in the phobic mothers of these children (in the context of a close identificatory system) is for the mother's symptomatic anxiety and avoidance behavior to arise as her daughter approaches mid-adolescence. The child begins to display (often as she is leaving school) a capacity for separation, involvement in the outside world and increasing sexual and aggressive behavior. In such households the daughter is often fearful of her own fantasies and impulses, and this finds concordance with the mother's renewed recognition within herself of similar wishes now being potentially lived out in her daughter. A fearful interaction takes place which leads to the daughter developing anorexia nervosa in order to avoid anxiety within herself and her mother. The issues at stake are as much those of protecting the mother and the whole family homeostasis as those of the patient avoiding these fears within her own fantasy life.

R. S. Kalucy, A. H. Crisp, and B. Harding, 1977
p. 392

Many Families Are Ill Equipped to Prepare Their Children for Adolescence

THERE ARE A number of families (but apparently not all) of anorectics who share certain features. An unusual interest in food, weight and shape, an unusual incidence of phobic avoidance and obsessive compulsive character traits, an unusual vulnerability to seemingly ordinary life events and a tendency to be unusually close, loyal and mutually interdependent. The common denominator of our description seems to us to be that these families are ill equipped for and prepare their children inadequately for the adolescent phase of development.

R. S. Kalucy, A. H. Crisp, and B. Harding, 1977
p. 394

The Child Is Ill Prepared for the
Demands of Adolescence

THE PARENTS GIVE the best of care, education and cultural exposure to the later anorectic child from whom they expect obedience and superior performance. By complying, the child fulfills the parents' dreams and compensates them for their own shortcomings, and family life is described as happy. Conditions change with adolescence. The child is ill prepared for the new demands, withdraws to her own body as the only realm where she can exercise control and dominance. Thus the illness begins.

Hilde Bruch, 1980
p. 256

The Mouth and Eating Are Especially Suitable for the
Representation of Ambivalence

AT NO PERIOD is the image of the body more charged or employed more in relation to psychic conflict than in adolescence. The inescapable need to integrate the representation of the sexually mature body into the eventual adult sexual organization is reflected in the prominence of the body image in the psychic life of the adolescent. In this process the image and functions of the body are all too readily available for the representation and experiencing of inner conflicts on the externalized screen of the body in the efforts at discharge, defense, and mastery. The mouth and eating offer rich possibilities because the oral cavity and its activities have a long history in the individual as both interoceptor and exteroceptor, facilitating both internalization and externalization in the mental processes that serve detoured discharge and defense in psychic conflict. That the mouth and eating serve both incorporation and expulsion make them especially suitable for the representation of ambivalence in which oral sadism is a major source of conflict.

Samuel Ritvo, 1980
p. 468

己

The Precipitating Factors Are Only Triggers and Not Truly Causative

THE PRECIPITATING factors in anorexia nervosa are only aleatory triggers to the surfacing of symptoms; they are not truly causative. Anorectics are sensitive to parental criticism and negative peer comments. They imagine insults. They cannot tolerate teasing, even with humor, and they take any critical remark in deadly earnest. A failure at school or at work sometimes appears to be a precipitant. Events that require decisions are difficult for anorectics. Menarche, sexual conflicts, and sexual confrontations in adolescence are powerful triggers, for they foster anxiety and regression. Comments about her face being "too fat" may have dire psychological consequences for the potential anorectic. Family snapshots of the anorectic, referring to her as a "cute, chubby baby," are upsetting. Death of a parent, loss through a divorce, or a move to a new neighborhood, with disruption from her close friends, can also be very upsetting to the anorectic. Physical illness of the mother, like a mastectomy with postoperative depression, can set off anorexia in a predisposed adolescent girl. A romantic rejection may plunge a young woman into gorging and vomiting.

John Sours, 1980
p. 275

己

Adolescents with True Anorexic Symptomatology Are People in Trouble

IT APPEARS THAT excessive concern about calories, weight, figure, diet, etc. has become extremely common, perhaps even normative, among adolescent females. Consequently, for that minority which finds the travails of adolescence too daunting it can readily be seized upon as a symptom choice. In this sense, anorexia nervosa has become a "fashionable" syndrome in an age consumed by thinness and, some would claim, by pathological narcissism. Again while we believe that all adolescents with true anorexic symptomatology, as opposed to an age-specific concern, are people in trouble, the sort and extent of trouble can vary greatly.

William Swift and Steven Stern, 1982
p. 22

Feelings of Resentment, Anger, and Rebellion May Be Stifled until Adolescence

BASICALLY PARENTS of anorexics and bulemics are quite concerned about the health and well-being of their children and will make great efforts to help them get well. Unwittingly, however, their excessive concern for their children beginning in infancy contributes to major problems over dependency and control. The parents are usually excessively attached to the child and foster an undue dependence upon the mother, which interferes with the child's growth and development, especially in the areas of separation and independence. The child is too clinging, fearful of being away from the mother, and imbued with an excessive need to be good, obedient, and perfect. The parents also exercise an undue degree of control over the child's behavior and inhibit progressive independent functioning. The child is able to stifle feelings of resentment, anger, and rebellion during most of childhood, which remain latent until the period of adolescence. At this time the increased aggressive drives and the characteristic psychic instability combine to topple the previously smooth functioning with a decompensation, releasing the anorexia syndrome. The child who cannot control relations with parents, friends, and interests at play and school begins to control food intake, body weight, exercise, and academic content.

C. Philip Wilson and Ira Mintz, 1982
p. 525

己

Starvation Diminishes the Changes of Adolescence

IT IS GENERALLY accepted that great anxiety over adolescent sexual changes—development of curves of the hips, legs, and breasts—contributes to the frequency of the disease at this point in time. Starvation and weight loss diminish these changes and give the patient the appearance of a preadolescent child.

Ira Mintz, 1983c
p. 93

己

Self-Starvation Serves as an Affirmation of Discipline and Self-Determination

IT IS [THESE] very hallmarks of pubertal adaptation and adult psychological health—the formation of a stable self-structure, tolerance of ambiguity and emotional intensity, and increasing plasticity of cognitive-psychological functioning—that are absent, or at least incompletely formed or consolidated, in the anorexic teenager. Against the backdrop of inhibited self-expression and the unstinting pursuit of external recognition, adolescence imposes heavy challenges and adds new burdens to vulnerability already sensed. In the face of these pressures, maturation is viewed as painfully disruptive and intrusive—a further catalyst to fears of exploitation and control by outside elements. Thus, however ruthless and brutalizing it may seem to others, self-starvation is positively valued: it serves as an affirmation of discipline and self-determination, and dampens threatening signals of physical change, and greatly simplifies matters of existence.

Michael Strober and Joel Yager, 1984
p. 366

The Struggle for Independence Revives
Intensely at Puberty

THE GIRL'S AMBIVALENT struggle for individuation and autonomy
from the mother persists long past the oedipal phase and revives
intensely at puberty, with its pressures towards physical and psychosocial maturation. The daughter's push towards independence frequently also triggers the mother's unresolved conflicts over separation
and loss derived from her relationship with her own mother. She fears
to lose the symbiotic, nurturing relation with her daughter and is
often unconsciously threatened by the girl's growing sexual attractiveness. Yet at the same time her own narcissism is heavily invested in her
daughter's appearance and social (and other) success, which leaves
both in a difficult "double bind."

Such conflicts are resolved in most women to the extent that the
positive aspects of the identificatory tie with the mother outweigh the
ambivalent, negative ones, although most adult women have greater
difficulties with autonomy and the need for attachment and intimacy
than do men. When the mother–daughter relationship is overly close
and hostile–dependent, when the mother unconsciously refuses to let
go and the daughter is unable to achieve actual or psychological
separation or a distinct identity of her own, then the stage is set for
many types of psychopathology. Depression and eating disorders are
among the most common of these, and often go together.

Hilary J. Beattie, 1988
p. 455

The Anorexic Enters Adolescence Bound to a
Possessive Mother

IT IS THUS—bound to a possessive mother who treats her as a mere
appendage and never as an individual deserving uncritical support—
that the patient enters adolescence and is faced with what to her is an
unbearable traumatic situation. She has to withdraw her libidinal

cathexis from the parental figures and to face the difficult problem of establishing new interpersonal relationships.

Mara Selvini Palazzoli, 1988
p. 160

己

Psychotherapy Presents Special Difficulties for Anorexic Adolescents

T HE FOLLOWING facts must be borne in mind especially:

1. The patients are generally minors, and as such economically and otherwise dependent on their parents.

2. The treatment is paid for by the parents, so that the therapist appears a mere hireling of people who often complain of the great expense, thus adding to the patients' guilt feelings, or as someone who turns on warmth and sympathy for financial gain.

3. The patients do not themselves choose psychotherapy. Generally they submit to it because they think the alternative—hospitalization or tube-feeding—is infinitely worse.

4. At adolescence children attempt to escape from the dominance of their elders, yet paradoxically the psychotherapeutic situation seems to resurrect and, indeed, even to increase their dependence on others.

5. Last but not least, because anorexics are afraid of verbalizing their conflicts and negative feelings, they tend to act them out by intensifying their symptom.

The therapist must bear all these points constantly in mind and, during crises, try to draw attention to them in simple and sympathetic ways.

Mara Selvini Palazzoli, 1988
p. 172

己

Characteristics of the Therapeutic Relationship

T HE MOVEMENT toward health entails forming a therapeutic relationship in which the anorexic can identify and express feelings, experience the empathic, nonjudgmental understanding of another person, separate from a pathological family system, resolve hostile dependent attachment to parents, assuage primitive guilt, and engage in the trials of adolescent psychosexual development to enter adulthood with the beginnings of a firm, cohesive sense of self.

Eugene Beresin, Christopher Gordon, and
David B. Herzog, 1989
p. 103

🮱

Any Loss Leaves the Adolescent Highly Vulnerable

W OMEN WITH future eating disorders, while appearing to function in a similar manner to normal adolescents, do not experience themselves as existing in a milieu that resonates with the potential for empathic support. The loss of a best friend does not lead, after a period of sadness to the relatively confident expectation of finding others who can perform similar selfobject functions; rather the loss is experienced as a drying up of the archaic selfobject environment. For future eating-disorder patients, the adolescent's environmental surround remains the "external provisional psychic structure" that has yet to be transmuted into internal capacities. Any loss leaves the adolescent highly vulnerable to the reemergence of disintegrating anxiety and the accompanying fear of emptiness.

Richard Geist, 1989
p. 21

🮱

For the Anorexic-to-be, Puberty Is
Profoundly Threatening

F OR THE ANOREXIC-TO-BE, the onset of puberty and menarche are profoundly disturbing. Her shaky sense of self-esteem and her intense need to comply with her mother's wishes make separation from the family threatening. Her fearful anticipation of criticism, rigid formulas, and black-and-white thinking compromise her ability to join the tumultuous peer group of other adolescents. The world seems unmanageable, hostile—she has no place to be safe.

Christopher Gordon, Eugene Beresin, and David Herzog, 1989
p. 39

◲

Anorexia Is a Reversal of Adolescence

THE GIRL'S RELATIONSHIP with her mother and father gives her little comfort as she takes on the role of young adult in her family. The relationship with her mother has been based on the child's compliance with her mother's need for a perfect child; in the face of multiplying appetites and urges and the normal adolescent impulse toward rebelliousness and dysphoria, the relationship with her mother offers no guidelines. Her father's attitude toward adult women makes female maturity a frightening prospect. For the anorexic-to-be, the solution is the reversal of adolescence, separation, and mature sexuality by self-starvation.

Christopher Gordon, Eugene Beresin, and David Herzog, 1989
p. 39

◲

Regression to Prepubertal Hormonal Levels

ANOREXIA NERVOSA is a disease that turns its victims against nature and, even, against life itself. Along with the repudiation of nutritional needs, which poses a threat to individual survival, goes a repudiation of sexuality in terms of psychological interest and physiological functioning, resulting in major interference with reproduction. For females, who make up 90–95% of anorectics, there is regression to prepubertal or pubertal levels of hormones, manifested in amenorrhea. Studies of male anorectics show a similar loss of sexual interest and potency and regression also to prepubertal or pubertal hormonal levels.

S. Louis Mogul, 1989
p. 65

The Tomboy May Feel Suddenly Bereft of Mirroring Responsiveness

ADOLESCENCE CAN bring with it further insults to the girl's exhibitionism. Girls at this age suddenly learn that from now on they will be expected to behave according to new rules, rules that may seem foreign and incomprehensible. They are asked to develop new ways of talking and moving their bodies, their hands, their eyes, their mouths in order to make themselves "attractive" to males. They learn that much of the way they may have been—forthright, strong, "natural"— is not attractive to males. They are asked to give up much of what may have provided the basis of their self-esteem and to take on a new way of being for which they feel woefully unequipped. The "tomboy"—who may have received a great deal of admiration from peers for her adventurousness and boldness—may feel suddenly bereft of mirroring responsiveness.

Susan Sands, 1989
p. 78

Adolescence Colludes with Anorexia

THE FACT THAT the illness may first appear in adolescence is often misleading. However, adolescence with its new defense formation against body changes, identity conflicts, and loss of object, colludes with the illness.

Marjorie P. Sprince, 1989
p. 76

The Dilemmas of Adolescence Bring the Dormant Pathology into View

As THE CONJUGATOR of childhood and adulthood, adolescence is always a battleground on which the past and future contend for the soul of the individual. With the anorectic, the necessity to integrate genital functioning into one's gender identity induces a profound regression that arrests the individual in the past, blocking any potential movements into adulthood. If the biological changes of pubescence had not taken place, the dormant illness of infancy might not have revealed itself. If it were not for the psychological trials of adolescence, we might never have known that this best of all little girls, provided with every advantage by her consciously well-intentioned family, had been subjected to a little soul murder and had been deprived of the authenticity of her being.

Until her changing body forced her to negotiate the dilemmas entailed in growing up from childhood to adulthood, the pathology in the anorectic's infantile history barely showed. In fact, as her parents were proud of announcing to everyone, she was good, clean, neat, polite, well behaved, delicate, cheerful and charming, smart in a dutiful, obedient way, but never challenging or controversial—the perfect feminine type.

Louise Kaplan, 1991
p. 459

The *Bête Noire* of the Anorectic Is Her Awakening Erotic Longing

For BOTH PARENTS, this chosen girl gets the rewards of love and admiration from her ability to follow rules and control her desires. What is such a girl to do when she arrives at puberty and every sight, sound, and movement reminds her of sexual desire? The *bête noire* of the anorectic is her awakening erotic longing. If her desires were to surface, the entire family would be destroyed. There is a solution. Perhaps if there were *no* desire in the self. . . ? Perhaps the physical body with its cravings so constantly excited by the phenomenal world could be mortified or obliterated? With her all-consuming interest in eating and not-eating, the anorectic is pretending that the last things on her mind are sex and genitals. This holier than thou, self-abnegating child is far too virtuous to entertain erotic thoughts or feelings.

Louise Kaplan, 1991
p. 464

8

Eating Disorders in Males

Anorexia as a Means to Control the Drives

MR. A WAS ENGAGED in an intense and exclusive relationship with a young woman his own age during his first year away from home. In the course of the year he became dependent on her in much the same way he had been dependent on his mother. He relied on her presence to calm him in academic stress situations just as he had relied on his mother to soothe and reassure him in such situations. The constant companionship of the girlfriend also served to shield him from the danger of homosexual feelings. Afflicted by obsessive thoughts and compulsive rituals since his latency years, he came for treatment a few weeks after his girlfriend abruptly broke off the relationship. He became seclusive, hypochondriacal, anorexic, severely compulsive, ritualistic, panicky, and nearly paralyzed in his academic work, turning to his mother once more and to the analyst for reassurance and supportive assistance to mobilize himself. The severe restriction of his eating became part of a monastic, ascetic, solitary existence in which food was a temptation to be avoided and all bodily appetites were to be extinguished. He limited his food to a minimal amount of milk products and a type of baked goods which either his mother supplied or he could obtain locally from a source identified with a woman. When, in the course of the analysis, his eating difficulty diminished, he was able to be aware of his anger at the young woman for abandoning him and eventually to be aware also of the negative side of his ambivalence toward his mother who had repeatedly been remote and unavailable because of her self-absorption and depression. The anger at her for her remoteness also served as a defense against his libidinal attachment to her. In shifting the focus of the conflict over his sexual and aggressive fantasies and aims to his body and food, the ego found an object for the drives in the body and eating functions. The shift was in the service of the effort to gain a measure of control over the drives by focusing on a different manifestation and derivative of the drives.

Samuel Ritvo, 1980
p. 456

⊐

Male and Female Anorexics Are Clinically Similar

MALE ANORECTICS differ in some respects from their female counterparts. Usually their disturbance begins in prepuberty; dauntless dieters, they are fearful of fatness, femininity, and sexuality. A later onset, usually with gorging and vomiting, is toward the end of secondary school, prior to college. They plunge into rigid starvation, usually with bulimia and vomiting, are extremely hyperactive and often rapidly lose weight. In general, however, male anorectics are clinically similar to female patients.

John Sours, 1980
p. 225

⊐

Incidence of Anorexia Is Lower in Males

BOYS DO NOT experience cultural pressure to be slim; instead, to be fit and strong. With puberty a boy's body does not add adipose tissue in the breasts, thighs, and hips; if concerned about obesity, it is his body in general that worries him. Fatness, to the boy, unless he labors with gender confusion, does not mean femininity and pregnancy—rather, it connotes weakness, passivity, and babyishness. It can also mean, decidedly so in adult men, strength, power, and dominance. Male puberty occurs later and less abruptly than it does in girls—when boys are more prepared for adolescence, are encouraged by their mother to detach, and are given more freedom, from the very beginning of infancy, to express aggression more openly. Their friends and gangs encourage them further. Likewise, pubertal changes for boys heighten self-assertion and aggression, direct the aggressive energy outward in the service of imposing force and control on others.

John Sours, 1980
pp. 271–272

Anorexia in Males Has the Same Features Presented by Women

PREMORBID FEATURES (in males) include childhood obesity, parental overprotection, excessive obedience, and a family setting with considerable strife and instability. Usually the anorexic managed to maintain a precarious psychic equilibrium until the stresses of preadolescence and adolescence proper destabilized it. Obesity and excessive preoccupation with food in family members were not unusual.

The syndrome itself is characterized by the same features presented by women: a conscious refusal of foods, especially carbohydrates; a deliberate pursuit of thinness; difficulty in recognizing emaciation and other body-image difficulties; vomiting and purging; and a preoccupation with diets and cooking . . . As is the case with female patients, these male patients had controlling mothers whose behavior toward them arose from the mothers' needs rather than in response to the needs of the children.

Ira Mintz, 1983b
p. 263

Need to Avoid Confrontation with the Powerful
Mother of Childhood

AFTER SIX MONTHS of treatment, Thomas described repeated episodes where the mother interfered with his attempts to separate and act independent. He would attempt to assert himself, fail, protest weakly, and then regress to anorexic behavior. These events took place when Thomas wanted to change the appearance of his room, expressed the wish for more privacy, and asked to use the family car more frequently, but in a realistic fashion. He spoke of his running as "running to be free," not just to burn up calories. In the midst of an argument with the mother after Thomas had gained 16 lbs., she yelled, "You're no better! You look thinner than when you started! You're not going to that therapist anymore."

At the end of the first year, Thomas was able to recover early memories of force-feeding—sitting in the tub for hours, crying, angry, and refusing to get out because mother would force him to drink chocolate milk; not leaving the table because he would have to drink his orange juice first; and spilling his milk out, but putting a ring of milk around his mouth with his finger to deceive her.

This vignette illuminates one probable origin of the almost universal deceitfulness in both male and female anorexics: the need to avoid an open confrontation with and defiance of the powerful mother of childhood out of fear of terrible retaliatory damage. Indeed, Thomas was still quite fearful of confronting his parents.

Ira Mintz, 1983b
p. 283

Lower Reported Prevalence of Eating
Disorders in Men

ANOREXIA NERVOSA involves greater psychopathology and carries a worse prognosis in males than in females. It is possible that those findings reflect the reluctance of all but the most severely ill males to request treatment. Our data, while preliminary and involving a small sample, point to a constellation of sexual difficulties—sexual isolation, inactivity, and conflicted homosexuality—that may complicate eating disorders in men. The reluctance of males to seek help for these stereotypically female disorders may be compounded by shame or anxiety in acknowledging conflicted, ambivalent attitudes about sexuality to a professional. This assumption, together with the fact that men suffer no symptom analogous to secondary amenorrhea (which often calls attention to these disorders in women), may partly explain the markedly lower reported prevalence of eating disorders in men.

David Herzog, Dennis Norman, Christopher Gordon, and
Maura Pepose, 1984
p. 990

Men Are Embarrassed about Having an Eating Disorder Associated with Being Female

W HY DO SO FEW male patients with bulimia appear for treatment? It appears that a gender difference in the prevalence of the disorder may not account for all of the discrepancy between the incidences of men and women seeking help for this problem. It may be that females with bulimia are more likely than males to seek treatment. Bulimia is frequently thought to be a "women's disease," and most of the men in our group expressed embarrassment about having an eating disorder associated with being female in the minds of most people.

J. Mitchell and G. Goff, 1984
p. 913

Unconscious Fantasy of Needing to Overeat or Die

M R. M WAS A middle-aged businessman who had been in treatment several times before I met him. He complained of a discrepancy between his intelligence and his capacities and his much lower level of performance. He consistently created situations which made things go wrong after he and I had worked to improve his life. He came from a large, poor family where education ranked high. He loved learning, but he could not integrate his efforts because he erotized his professional activities. He engaged in certain perversions, predominantly a type of pedophilia, and he was bulimic. The perversion and bulimia compelled him to interrupt his work and then to live in terror of discovery.

This behavior had its roots in his earliest history, of which only *one* aspect can be reported here. He was told that he almost died shortly after birth because of a milk allergy. He had an organizing screen memory in which he was two-and-a-half to three years old. His mother had put him on top of a bedroom dresser. He was fat, had round cheeks and they smiled at each other. She was feeding him. They were both laughing and were happy together.

In actuality, his mother force-fed him as long as he could remember. He had a weight problem and found her force-feeding increasingly intrusive, but he shared mother's fantasy that he might die if he did not eat everything she served him. Because of his lifelong anxiety that he might die, he could not fend her off.

During analysis, this theme was relived—initially by a bout of insomnia during which he raided the icebox, gained several pounds overnight, and jogged them off within the next twenty-four hours. He always enumerated what he had eaten, and when it included entire cakes and quarts of ice cream, I became concerned.

After several years of work, during which the patient accused me of not helping him and of interpreting things he already knew, he developed nightmares. They were wordless, but he felt in terror and totally alone. He asked to sit up. He did so and held his head in his hands, feeling unable to look at me. He complained about the light in the room and I realized he had developed a photophobia. I had to draw the shades and close them tightly. We worked this way for months, often sitting in silence.

When he began to talk, the patient said he could not bear to be touched. I told him that I thought he reacted like a person who was beginning to remember having been overstimulated intolerably to the point of feeling that if it continued, he would perish. Working on this theme helped him to connect his fear of the light in the room with the fear of being intrusively force-fed by mother and with his fear of death. Certain aspects of the pedophilia could also be understood: he became the mother who "force-fed" a child by penetrating its body. His genital stood for the force-feeding spoon and the little girl represented himself. But a theme of merging with mother and excluding father was also most prominent.

In his perverse activities as well as in his bulimic behavior, the patient unconsciously shared a fantasy with his mother that unless he compulsively overate or intruded sexually upon a young person's body (who then would feel overfed), he would perish. Both eating and pedophilia staved off death and were based on sexualized and destructive unconscious needs and wishes, including death wishes against mother. Excessive guilt was associated with the destructive aspects of the bulimia and pedophilia and a constant fear of being caught.

The influence of the mother had been so predominant in this case because the father disappeared from Mr. M's life when he was still a very young child. His siblings were no protection against his menacing mother.

The photophobia had represented a displaced wish of shutting out his intrusive mother, who was represented by the incoming light. As memories from childhood appeared, the nightmares became less frequent and the patient gradually gained autonomy over his eating habits and impulse control over his perversion. As he struggled to gain autonomy and to separate from mother, his phallic and oedipal needs emerged in treatment. Conflicts preventing productive work gradually moved to the area of intrapsychic conflict and could be analyzed. He gradually became the arbiter of his own destiny.

Maria Bergmann, 1988
p. 365

ㄹ

Ten to Fifteen Percent of All Bulimics Are Males

AN EXTENSIVE SEARCH of the English-language literature on bulimia in males revealed that the disorder affects approximately 0.2 percent of adolescent boys and young adult men and that males account for 10–15 percent of all bulimic persons identified in community-based studies.

Daniel Carlat and Carlos Camargo, Jr., 1991
p. 840

⊇

It Is More Socially Acceptable for a Man to Exercise to Excess

BECAUSE CULTURAL pressure to be thin, a factor for many eating-disordered women, may be less severe for men, clinicians, parents, and physicians may fail to identify as bulimic the many male bulimics who are overweight. In addition, bulimic men may not be readily diagnosed who, although not vomiting or restricting their food intake, exercise excessively to stay thin. It is more socially acceptable for a man to exercise to excess than for a woman.

John Schneider, 1991
p. 196

⊇

There Is a Range of Gender-Identity Issues in Male Eating Disorders

I SUGGEST THAT IN most cases of male eating disorders, there is some form of gender identity concern—sometimes more dramatic, as in cases of core gender identity problems, and sometimes less obvious, as in cases of gender role identity problems. Most bulimic men have disturbances in core gender identity and/or severe difficulty in masculine identification.

John Schneider, 1991
p. 204

己

Bulimia as an Attempt to Define Oneself as Masculine

Mr. s, 26 years old, came to treatment because he "felt stuck." He said, "I don't know where to turn – I'm unhappy with the environment I'm living in." He was tall and thin with a deep voice and a crew cut, looking much younger than his age.

S had a bingeing ritual that involved eating a large breakfast and then going to several secret trails he had laid out, where he vomited and jogged. He repeated the same routine in the afternoon. He felt physically weak and drained after these episodes. Although he felt the routine was degrading, he said that he repeated it out of boredom and feelings of anger and deprivation.

S said that he had been concerned about his body most of his life – at age 9 about having a fat stomach, by age 12 about his weight. As a child he hated school, and missed up to 14 weeks every year for various somatic complaints for which no cause was found. He looked forward to the time alone with his mother and the special meals she would make for him. (He was the youngest of several children.)

S's mother had a secret drinking problem that she denied, although S felt that her personality was changed by it and that it caused problems with his father. She used heavy denial as well as alcohol to deal with her depression. His father never confronted his mother about the problem; it was S who eventually confronted her, and he stayed out of school to try to cure her. He was desperate to stay at home, perhaps out of fear that she would die without him.

In high school he worked on bodybuilding. His first 2 years at a local college went well enough, except for his concerns about his appearance. He lost weight the summer before transferring to an out-of-state college, and felt that people were noticing his skinniness, which made him feel he was more in control than other people. While he was away at college, his eating got out of control; he went from 160 to 200 pounds in 5 weeks. He did not make a college athletic team, although he was quite skilled. He had trouble concentrating on his schoolwork, and after 9 weeks, he dropped out and returned home.

At the time of our first meeting he was also concerned about his

severe difficulty in getting along with his father. He had been living
with his father, cooking for him, and sporadically working odd jobs.
S's father worked 7 days a week, 12 hours a day, at a food-related job
that S felt was menial. S despised his father's ordinary life and
"establishment" values, and said, "I never wanted to be like that and
follow what the norm was." Deeply saddened by his mother's death,
he was equally hopeful that he would have more time with his father.
His anticipation turned to disappointment, perhaps because instead
of becoming a son, he took the place of his mother in the house-
hold.

My understanding of S's issues is that he suffered from a severe
separation anxiety that had continued throughout his life. S identified
with his mother as a means of remembering her (rather than
mourning her loss), and wished to hang onto her as an undifferen-
tiated object. His bulimia was a way of continuing his mother's
alcoholism. She had also had an eating disorder when she was a child.
As do many patients with separation problems, S felt he was being left
behind when all the other (and older) children left. Like some
youngest children, he tried to cure his depressed mother by not
separating from her.

S's father was a weak and psychologically absent individual who
worked all the time and did not take his place to help his son
"triangulate" out of his early relationship with his mother. Like his
mother, who attempted to humiliate her husband for not being
a "good provider," S also had a distaste for what he perceived as
his father's ineffectual masculine role, and became confused about his
own gender role identity. He seemed to have assumed his mother's role
in the family: staying home, cooking for his father, and being jealous
of his father, just as the mother had been jealous and insisted on
including herself in their father–son activities.

S's bulimia appeared to be his attempt to define himself as masculine in an external, physical way to counter his internal doubts and
fears of merger with mother. His bingeing and vomiting were a
defensive means to justify staying with the mother, a futile effort to
repair his disturbance in masculinity. Exercising was a way to com-
pensate for his passivity, and he said it made him feel "strong,
masculine, and in control." His identity appeared to be in limbo: he
was unable either to move away from his mother or to move toward

his father and a masculine role. His life was on hold. Socially he never had boyfriends or girlfriends and was unable to enter the academic or work world, staying at home instead to keep the image of his mother alive by assuming her role.

John Schneider, 1991
p. 207

9

Family Dynamics

Parents Think that Not Eating Is the Only Problem

ANOREXICS ... ARE more determined than all other mental patients to cling on to a symptom they have been protecting tooth and nail against attacks from all sides and particularly from their parents, who think that once they start eating properly all the remaining problems will vanish by themselves.

Mara Selvini Palazzoli, 1963
p. 112

⊒

Parents and the Patients May Present a Glowing
Picture of a Perfect Family

NOT ONLY THE parents but the patients too, when first seen, are apt to give a glowing picture of the blessings and happiness of their home, that the anorexia is the only flaw in what otherwise would be a perfect life. Some of this is a direct denial of facts, or a fear of being put in the position of saying something critical. It is also an expression of overconformity: what the parents said was always right and they blamed themselves for not being good enough.

Hilde Bruch, 1978
p. 32

One Never Knows in Whose Name Anyone Is Speaking

A COMMON FEATURE is that the future patient was not seen or acknowledged as an individual in her own right, but was valued mainly as someone who would make the life and experiences of the parents more satisfying and complete. Such expectations do not preclude a relationship of great warmth and affection. Usually clinging attachment and a peculiarly intense sharing of ideas and feelings develop. When seen together as a family, it is rare that any one member speaks in direct terms about his or her own ideas and feelings. Each one seems to know what the other feels and truly means, at the same time disqualifying what the other has said. I have called this style of communication a "confusion of pronouns" because one never knows in whose name anyone is speaking.

Hilde Bruch, 1978
p. 36

Parents Are Unaware of Their Excessive Control

THESE PARENTS speak with conviction of their approach to life as right, normal, and desirable, and of their being entitled to expect that this child will fulfill their dreams and wishes. The child's inability for constructive self-assertion and the associated deficits in personality development are the outcome of interactional patterns that began early in life. The parents' unawareness that they have exercised such excessive control over the child and their inability to let go of it are part of the on-going pattern that sustains the illness.

Hilde Bruch, 1978
p. 38

The Brightest, Sweetest, and Most Obedient
Child Ever

EVERY ONE OF HER teachers told me what a joy it was to have her in her room." With this sentence the mother of an 18-year-old anorexic girl began the interview. Another brought a note from the teacher of her 12-year-old anorexic daughter, "A sweeter, smarter little lady would be difficult to find." They, and many other parents, value such testimonials because they support their own convictions that the miserable, angry, and desperate patient had been the best, brightest, sweetest, most obedient, and most cooperative child ever.

Hilde Bruch, 1978
p. 40

A Parent Watcher

SINCE THE EVALUATION of what she does is another's domain, the child develops an obsessive concern for perfection. She is both extremely conscious of herself and keenly alert to other people's signals. She is a parent watcher.

S. Minuchin, B. L. Rosman, and L. Baker, 1978
p. 59

Loyalty and Protection Take Precedence over
Autonomy and Self-Realization

THE ANORECTIC child has grown up in a family operating with highly enmeshed patterns. As a result, her orientation toward life gives prime importance to proximity in interpersonal contact. Loyalty and protection take precedence over autonomy and self-realization. A child growing up in an extremely enmeshed system learns to subordinate the self. Her expectation from a goal-directed activity, such as studying or learning a skill, is therefore not competence, but approval. The reward is not knowledge, but love.

S. Minuchin, B. L. Rosman, and L. Baker, 1978
p. 59

⊒

Control Is Maintained under the Cloak of Concern

THE CHILD'S AUTONOMY is curtailed by the intrusive concern and overprotection of other family members. Large areas of her psychological and bodily functioning remain the subject of others' interest and control long after they should have become autonomous. This control is maintained under the cloak of concern, so that the child cannot challenge it. Since family members make their wishes known indirectly and unselfishly—"I want this because it is good for you"— disagreement and even initiative become acts of betrayal. The denial of self for another's benefit and family loyalty are highly valued. The concern for mutual accommodation without friction produces an environment in which differences are denied and submerged.

S. Minuchin, B. L. Rosman, and L. Baker, 1978
p. 59

⊒

Anorectic Families Focus on Bodily Functions

IT IS CHARACTERISTIC of anorectic families, as well as of psychosomatic families in general, to focus on bodily functions. Many family members present somatic complaints. Such complaints can represent either bona-fide illness or merely general sensitivity to normal physiological processes. In families with an anorectic child, the entire family often has a special concern with such matters as eating, table manners, diets, and food fads.

S. Minuchin, B. L. Rosman, and L. Baker, 1978
p. 61

〓

Paucity of Confirmation of Child-Initiated Clues

T HE OUTSTANDING finding in the early development of anorectics is the paucity of confirmation of child-initiated clues. In these families growth and development are not conceived of as the child's accomplishment but as that of the parents.

Hilde Bruch, 1980
p. 257

〓

Families Are Poor Historians

T HEY AND THEIR families are very poor historians. It is impossible to obtain from them more than global descriptions of events. Their life appears as a colorless continuation of routine events. From the patients one hears of their performing for others, attempting to be perfect, longing to be recognized and seen, and feeling totally impotent to influence others; from the parents one senses that they have not noticed anything unusual in the child but see only happiness, good behavior, average development, and, after decompensation, incomprehensible stubbornness.

Ana-Maria Rizzuto, Ross K. Peterson, and
Marilyn Reed, 1981
p. 478

〓

The Anorexic Puzzles and Infuriates the Family

THE ANOREXIC'S behavior is puzzling and eventually becomes infuriating to those around her who are reduced to helplessness in the face of her intransigence. She wounds those nearest her by rejecting all they have to offer her. To them, her persistent refusal to eat seems like the epitome of perversity: she is choosing death rather than life, sickness rather than health or, at best, a narrow existence in preference to a full one. They can see no reasons for her behavior. But of course there are reasons, many of them too close to home to be seen by those involved.

Sheila MacLeod, 1982
p. ix

〓

Parents' Anxiety Leads to the Need to Control the Child

THE PARENTS' NEED to control the anorexic child is remarkably strong and tenaciously adhered to; it arises from parents' anxiety over loss of control over the environment, of which the child is an integral part. It does not necessarily arise from dislike for the child, but may result from the parents' attempt to cope with threatening aspects of their own personality, or from a childhood relationship displaced onto the current child.

Ira Mintz, 1983c
p. 97

〓

Overconscientiousness Leads to Overcontrol

IT IS HEALTHY for a child to grow up in a home where there are rules, limits, and a parental example of impulse control, responsibility, and ethical behavior; however, in their *over*conscientiousness, the parents of anorexics *over*control their child.

C. Philip Wilson, 1983b
p. 30

己

Overconscientious Perfectionism

T HE OVERCONSCIENTIOUS perfectionism of the parents in these families resulted in infantilizing decision-making and overcontrol of the children. In some of the families, fun for fun's sake was not allowed. Everything had to have a noble purpose; the major parental home activity was intellectual discussion and scholarly reading. It was no surprise that the anorexic daughters hated the long hours of study they felt compelled to do. In therapy, it was difficult for them to become independent and mature and to get rid of the humiliating feeling that they were puppets whose strings were pulled by their mother and father.

C. Philip Wilson, 1983b
p. 31

己

P*R*I*D*E*S

T HE PSYCHOLOGICAL profile of the anorexic family should guide the therapist's interviews with the family. A useful acronym for the profile is PRIDES. P = perfectionism, R = repression of emotions, I = infantilizing decisionmaking for the anorexia-prone child, D = parental overconcern with dieting and fears of being fat, E = sexual and toilet exhibitionism, S = the selection of one child for the development of anorexia.

C. Philip Wilson, 1983b
p. 33

己

The Child Is Treated by Each Parent as a Self Object

W E HAVE FOUND that she is forced by each parent to reflect his or her specific facade and to aid each in his or her defense against true feelings. In short, the child is treated by each parent as a self object, utilized to maintain the inner psychic harmony of the parent. The result is that the child is not allowed to form a true, spontaneous self but is channeled into an existence which is justified only to the extent that it bolsters the defenses while it also secretly mirrors the needs of each parent.

Jules Bemporad and John Ratey, 1985
p. 458

Parents Unavailable as Soothing, Calming Objects

T HE ANORECTIC patient's retrospective perceptions suggest a chronic dearth of parental availability as idealizable models with whose soothing, calming, omnipotent presence she would have been able to merge. Rather, she perceives her parents as having been intrusively panicky in response to anxiety signals. For example, an anorectic adolescent attending college in a distant state telephoned her mother following an argument with a roommate. Anxious and upset, she told her mother about the petty quarrel, then added that she hated her dorm, her teachers, and her courses and that she intended to transfer schools. Mother interrupted saying, "Oh, wait till your father hears this; he'll be so upset. I just don't know what to do with you. Wait till I check my schedule and see when I can fly out and talk to the right people and straighten this out for you." Instead of responding to the patient with a calm and reassuring presence, a holding environment which contains the patient's anxiety, the young woman perceives the parental reaction as chronically exacerbating her anxiety through the unwittingly communicated theme: you are helpless and need us to solve your problems.

Richard Geist, 1985
p. 13

Contrary to Anorectic Families, Bulimic Families Do Not Appear to Be Perfect, Selfless, and Conflict-Avoidant

QUITE DISSIMILAR to the anorexics', the bulimics' families do not appear to be the perfect, selfless family that avoids conflict at all cost. On the contrary, the families of bulimics do experience subjective distress and conflict in their relationships with one another. The interaction patterns of bulimic families can also be overtly hostile, angry, and manipulative. Importantly, though, family members seem unable to express their negative feelings openly and directly; instead, they bicker, blame, and sulk about less central issues, sometimes endlessly, without ever being able to resolve the real conflict among them.

Thus, the bulimic provides a diversionary focus for both the enmeshed bickering and for the family's unified concern and help. This focus, negative and positive, on the bulimic child allows the family to avoid more dangerous, subterranean conflicts in the marriage. Typically, marital distress consists of a lack or loss of emotional intimacy, alcoholism, and/or depression. Such a pattern can be quite powerful in maintaining family stability even if the bulimic lives away from home because her parents can certainly continue to worry and argue together about her in her absence. Interestingly, the bulimic is often perceived as the "black sheep" of the family, despite her self-sacrifices for it. She is not so likely to be seen as the perfect daughter as is the anorexic.

Laura Lynn Humphrey, 1986
p. 315

The Impulsivity in the Bulimic Family Can Resemble the Bulimic's Binge

DESPITE THE FAMILY'S efforts to "diet," or restrict and control each other and themselves, their strong but unsatisfied needs for affection and acceptance compel them to keep striving. At times these drives and strivings can become so intense that they resemble the bulimic's binge. Family members may seek or demand immediate gratification or become impulsive and isolated. Their family boundaries can shift from hierarchical rigidity to being too loose and ineffectual. Similarly, what is overtly structured at one time may dissolve into virtual chaos at another. Perhaps most obviously, the affective expression among family members can be unmodulated and labile. Thus, the family's "binge" reflects a loss of self-regulation, effective relating, and an organizing structure to more basic needs and impulses.

Laura Lynn Humphrey, 1986
p. 319

The Chaotic Bulimic Family

W HILE MANY THEORISTS and researchers have described eating-disordered families similar to the perfect family and the overprotective family, the chaotic family type frequently observed in bulimia has not been described in the literature on eating disorders. Instead, chaotic families, not often seen as the context for anorexia nervosa, resemble substance-abusing families . . . The experiences of children growing up in alcoholic families are similar to those of bulimics from chaotic families: they learn not to talk, trust, or feel.

While enmeshment and lack of conflict resolution skills exist in the chaotic family, as in the other two family types, many of the markers and signs of this family's patterns are distinct from the overprotective and the perfect family. For example, while the perfect and overprotective family types are hallmarked by their rigid rules, the chaotic family is hallmarked by the inconsistency of its rules. Other hallmarks of the chaotic family type are: unavailability of one or both parents, victimization experiences of the family member (or members), frequent expression of anger, and substance abuse.

Maria Root, Patricia Fallon, and William Friedrich, 1986
p. 112

To the Anorexic and Bulimic Child, Even Aggressive Thoughts Feel Like Acts of Disloyalty

IN FAMILIES OF anorexics and bulimics aggression for whatever purpose is not well tolerated, often resulting in the near total submerging of aggressive impulses and feelings. When the preanorexic or bulimic child expresses anger or defiance, the parents experience it as either a narcissistic injury, an intolerable expression of separateness, or an act of betrayal, and they respond accordingly such that the child learns that this is unacceptable behavior. Indeed, this prohibition may be internalized to the point that even having aggressive *thoughts* feels to the child like an act of disloyalty and is accompanied by guilt and fear.

Steven Stern, 1986
p. 247

Systematic Training in Dishonesty

IT IS READILY apparent to me that the so-called good or model phase in the later anorexic's life is the time when she experiences something that may be called systematic training in dishonesty. As a child she is praised and rewarded with approval for being "good" when she puts on a smiling and cheerful face. No attention is paid to the painful underlying misery, of which she too is scarcely aware.

Hilde Bruch, 1988
p. 11

The Insensitive Parent Interferes

DURING CHILDHOOD and the latency period, an insensitive parent constantly interferes, criticizes, suggests, takes over vital experiences, and prevents the child from developing feelings of his own.

Mara Selvini Palazzoli, 1988
p. 159

己

Both Parents' Needs Are Obscured by Apparent
Service to Others

In THESE FAMILIES, mother is typically extraordinarily giving, attentive
to the needs of everyone in the family, and perfectionistic in her strict
standards for her own behavior, yet she is inhibited in directly
asserting her own needs. She is more comfortable meeting the needs of
others, and regards self-sacrifice as the highest virtue. She communicates an ideal of womanhood as selfless and unindulgent of appetites of
any sort. Underneath her deference and solicitude to others, particularly to her husband, one senses impatience and resentment that are
not expressed, since to express such feelings would be self-indulgent.
Often she is married to a man who is as unable to give of himself as his
wife is unable to take for herself. The husband, uneasy with dependency on women, assuages his distrust of women by devaluing them
and by demanding unquestioning loyalty and deference from his wife
and children. Frequently, however, the father's demands are covered
over by an attitude of self-sacrifice or overwork. Both parents' needs
are then obscured by apparent service to others.

Christopher Gordon, Eugene Beresin, and David Herzog, 1989
p. 30

己

Paternal Narcissistic Entitlement

In MANY FAMILIES we have seen, the mother's deferentiality, solicitude,
and apparent generosity are matched by a complementary entitlement
to this behavior in the father. In some fathers this takes the form of
autocracy in decision making, ruling the family unilaterally; in others
it may take even more blatant forms, such as demanding the largest or
best serving of food. Many of these fathers are extremely successful in
their professional lives where indeed they may rule with just this sort
of authority. One frequently discerns beneath the professional success
and mastery of these men problems in self-esteem and basic trust that

are similar to their wives' issues: a needy, dependent, and frightened side, which is fiercely denied. These men distrust women, who are perceived as powerful in their capacity to betray and abandon, and often deal with their distrust by attempts to control and dominate women. These husbands are exquisitely sensitive to hidden resentment and hostility beneath their wives' reactive generosity. Again like their wives, these fathers often do not consciously acknowledge their needs, nor are they often confronted by their wives—at least those whom we are describing here—because their own deferentiality proscribes such self-assertion.

Christopher Gordon, Eugene Beresin, and David Herzog, 1989
p. 37

Preserve Harmony at Any Price

IN OUR FAST-MOVING age, the ability to develop requires partners to constantly redefine their own individual identities vis-à-vis each other, to accept conflict, to withstand disharmony and the tensions born of ambivalence, and at the same time to remain in constructive communication with one another. And this development is made extremely difficult, if not impossible, by marital relationships governed by the motto that one must not let oneself go, must preserve harmony, must respect conventions, and must stick together at any price.

Helm Stierlin and Gunthard Weber, 1989
p. 30

No Boundaries

SUCH A FAMILY reminds us of a house in which all the rooms are interconnected and all the doors are open. Frequently, this is quite literally the case: it is always possible for any member of the family to enter another's room—his or her private domain—without knocking. Often even the parents' bedroom will be left open and not have a lock on the door.

Helm Stierlin and Gunthard Weber, 1989
p. 31

⊐

Commandment of Selflessness

THE BLANKET "commandment of selflessness" will inevitably lead to rivalry over who gives more, sacrifices more, controls him/herself best, suppresses his/her own needs most effectively, and so on. Within such rivalry, any attempts at autonomy and self-realization will be branded as self-centeredness and then blocked in a process of reciprocal exacerbation. Anyone who takes a little more for him/herself than the others, and perhaps is a little more capable of pleasure and enjoyment than they are, is accused of letting him/herself go and taking the easy way out. Self-denial, by contrast, is a way of gaining prestige within the family.

Helm Stierlin and Gunthard Weber, 1989
p. 34

⊐

Anorexia: Proof of Parental Failure

THERE DEVELOPS A revenge dynamic, characteristic of bound delegates who come to realize that all the sacrifices they have made with a view to living up to their parents' expectations have been in vain. Typically, the most effective way they find to satisfy their vindictive feelings is by patterning their behavior in order to make their parents look like failures.

Helm Stierlin and Gunthard Weber, 1989
p. 47

No One in the Family Can Conscientiously
Nurture and Soothe

THE HOLDING environment in anorexic and bulimic families fails them in (1) nurturance, (2) soothing and tension regulation, and (3) empathy and affirmation of separate identities. Parents and children alike are "starving" for nurturance, through emotional warmth and tenderness, and genuine unconditional affection for one another. This deficit in nurturance is compounded by an equally deficient capacity to tolerate and regulate tension and negative affective states. Families of anorexics and bulimics are unable to modulate frustration, anxiety, painful impingements from the environment, or overstimulation from either internal or external sources, so that these states interfere with their goal-directed functioning. This occurs because there is a profound absence of anyone in the family who can nurture, soothe, and sustain such overwhelming affects on a consistent enough basis.

Laura Lynn Humphrey, 1991
p. 324

Failures in the Holding Environment Are
Multi-Generational

CLINICAL EXPERIENCE with anorexic and bulimic families suggests that these failures in the holding environment are family-wide and multi-generational. They do not begin with the parents, nor will they end with the bulimic or anorexic daughter. Instead, the deficits in nurturance, soothing, and individuation reflect a transgenerational, developmental arrest or fixation that these families are trying desperately to master. It is an intergenerational legacy, if you will. The parents were never nurtured, soothed, or empathized with by their own parents, so that each parent is forever trying to master the deficits through re-enactments with their spouse and children. They impose their own preoccupations and unmet needs on their children, who in turn take care of the parents and sacrifice themselves; thus the pattern repeats itself.

Laura Lynn Humphrey, 1991
p. 324

己

Differences between Anorexic and Bulimic Families

THESE DIFFERENCES (between anorexic and bulimic families) are not so much in the underlying deficits with which they struggle, but rather in their particular adaptations to these deficits. In anorexic families, for example, nurturance can be lavished on the daughter, but only so long as she remains totally dependent and childlike. Once she begins to separate, she is negated, abandoned, or punished for doing so. The situation is different in bulimic families, where there is more likely to be a generalized experience of insatiable "hunger" for loving affection throughout the family. Another difference lies in the ways these two types of families attempt to regulate tension and dysphoric affects. The anorexic's family is quite constricted, superficial, and denying, just as she is herself. By contrast, the bulimic's family is more chaotic, hostile, and understructured—with the exception of the bulimic's mother, who fluctuates between intense neediness and being overwhelmed on the one hand, and cold, embittered denial and withholding on the other.

Laura Lynn Humphrey, 1991
p. 325

己

Anorexia Is Soul Murder

ANOREXIA IS THE outcome of one of those little soul murders of childhood in which, to survive, a child gives up aspects of the self she might have become and instead becomes a mirroring extension of the all-powerful other on whom her life depended.

Louise Kaplan, 1991
p. 455

Some Families Act as if the Behavior Were Invisible

IT IS DIFFICULT to imagine that a young woman can become severely underweight or use invasive purging techniques like persistent vomiting and laxative abuse without creating high anxiety in her partner or family. Yet, the coping strategies that she and her intimates develop over time, in mutual accommodation, actually allow her behavior to occur without intervention. The result is that the family acts as if the behavior were invisible, despite the fact that the anorexic's eating can be highly ritualistic, obvious, and extremely disturbing.

Laura Giat Roberto, 1993
p. 7

10

Family Treatment

Parents Need Compassionate Understanding

Pᴀʀᴇɴᴛꜱ ɴᴇᴇᴅ ᴛᴏ be helped to a greater understanding of the problem, they need to grasp their own importance in the matter and to become involved. They need to construe their new roles reflecting their responsibilities rather than their blame. They need compassionate help, perhaps allowing them to see that we all have our Achilles' heel and that this just happens to be theirs as individuals and as a family.

Arthur H. Crisp, 1980
p. 99

Only Family Meetings Bring to the Surface the Basic Family System

Fᴀᴍɪʟʏ ᴛʜᴇʀᴀᴘʏ can be initially useful in delineating the disturbed, structured interactions that occur in these enmeshed families. It is most effective with young anorectics soon after the clinical onset of the disturbance. The more entrenched anorectic family, imbued with the mythic idea of superhuman performance and appearance, is less responsive. Its members are loath to reveal any family disturbance and pain. Their language is full of suggestions; it is a structure, a dialect called body metaphor, a dialect that has to be translated through treatment. Only family meetings bring to the surface the basic family system, its structure, function, communications, myths, metaphors, and pathology. Family therapy is drastic enough, in confrontations with family members, to bring the family system and pathology into bold relief, to lift up the anorectic to the point of buoyancy. The mother's narcissistic use of the anorectic child is immediately apparent, as is the inability of the family members to directly verbalize their own aggression. In cases where the anorectic disturbance is more oedipally colored, one can see the seductiveness of the hysterical father in the family sessions. In general, treating a young hospitalized patient without involving the family leads to a relapse when the family system is rejoined.

John Sours, 1980
p. 368

Direct Work with the Family and Individual Psychotherapy Complement Each Other

IN THE CLARIFICATION of the family involvement, direct work with the family and individual psychotherapy complement each other. Although family problems exist in the present, their resolution alone is not sufficient, since the patient has integrated the abnormal patterns and misconceptions of the past. Sufficient freedom from the family involvement needs to develop for a patient to become ready to explore her handicapping inner problems. The family members themselves need help and support to permit the young person greater freedom; they need help in particular with their anxiety so as to prevent premature interruption of treatment. Successful treatment implies changes in a patient so that she can become capable of adult living with greater independence and self-reliance. Parents often say, "If only she could be again the girl she was," overlooking the fact that "the girl she was" was unable to face growing up and adult living. The knowledge and understanding gained through work with the family gives the therapist important guidelines on what problems and issues to pursue in individual therapy.

Hilde Bruch, 1982b
p. 1535

ㄹ

Alter the Interaction that Supports the Patient's Lack of Reliance on Her Own Thoughts and Feelings

FAMILY THERAPY sessions are instrumental with many patients in altering the interactional patterns which have come to support the patient's lack of reliance on her own thoughts, emotions, perceptions, and behavior. The family's overinvolvement not only inhibits the development of autonomy but also endorses the patient's sense that her own functioning is inherently deficient. On one level the parents' taking care of every need bears the message of affection, but it may also sabotage the child's self-initiated behavior.

Paul Garfinkel and David Garner, 1982
p. 282

ㄹ

Warn Parents that with Improvement, Aggressive Behavior May Appear

THE PARENTS ARE warned that as the anorexia begins to subside, it may well be replaced by different behavior – depression, aggressive acting out, or other forms of aggression – which must be tolerated so as not to force the patient back into the anorexia.

Ira Mintz, 1983c
p. 97

ㄹ

When the Parents Can Relinquish Their Control, the Effect May Be Quite Remarkable

W HEN THE ANOREXIC child is in treatment, it is quite desirable, and often necessary, for the parents to see another therapist to be able to understand the nature of the illness in general and to learn what to do to facilitate the child's progress. When parents are able to recognize their need to control the child and then relinquish this control in a positive fashion, the effect on the child can be helpful and, occasionally, quite remarkable. When they are unable to relinquish control, progress can be markedly impaired. If the child makes progress in self-assertion and independence in the face of marked parental resistance, the parents' psychological stability can become impaired to the point of decompensation.

In general, it is feasible to see the parents together for about 6–10 consultations. During that time, one obtains a history of the anorexic syndrome and the developmental background that preceded it, along with an evaluation of the parents' problems, attitudes toward one another, and behavior toward the patient from birth onward.

The parents are told that the anorexia covers up major problems of independence, helplessness, aggression, and sexuality. It is indicated that the patient's endless preoccupation with food and eating in part is an attempt to control eating because the patient feels unable to control much else, and that the patient must learn to deal with the other aspects of life. Toward this end, the parents are encouraged to avoid all discussions of food. The more attention the parent pays to eating and food, the more the patient is encouraged to maintain the preoccupation with food, instead of dealing with the other major problems that have been avoided. At the same time, when the parents push the patient to eat, the patient derives a sense of sadistic satisfaction from not eating and from irritating the parents. The greater the sadistic gratification, the less willing the patient is to renounce it. Getting the parents to give up the concern over eating and food is a very difficult task, especially when they are confronted by a starving, emaciated, and provocative child.

Ira Mintz, 1983c
p. 97

⊐

Perfectionism in the Family of the Anorexic

THE RS CAME for consultation about their 17-year-old daughter, Sally, who six months earlier had started a diet that she then rigidly followed until she lost 30 lbs. and became anorexic. A hyperactive, overconscientious girl who got up at 5:00 A.M. to recheck her homework, Sally gave a history typical of anorexic adolescents. She always had been a good girl, obsessed with proper behavior, studying, and social achievement. The father, a 50-year-old successful business executive, grew up in Boston. Mr. R was very idealistic. He disapproved of the business world and always wished he could have become a physician. The care of the children was relegated to his wife. Mrs. R, a 45-year-old social worker, divided her time between a full-time career and her family. She was very ladylike and overconcerned with manners and proper behavior for her daughter. When faced with emotional situations or fights, she frequently developed skin rashes and hives. She was very afraid of being fat and nagged her husband, who was a few pounds overweight, to join her in dieting.

Sally's brother Robert, two years her senior, was an easygoing adolescent boy who had a succession of girlfriends, smoked, drank, and enjoyed parties, dancing, and rock music. Although the mother weakly argued with Robert and chided him for his poor school performance, most of her attention was focused on her daughter. She did everything she could for Sally, helping her with her studies, reviewing her homework, and barraging her with advice and criticism.

The Rs followed a strict regime: meals were always on time, television was rationed at one hour a day, and the major parental relaxation was intellectual discussion and serious reading. The parents never quarreled in front of their children and in general shared the same ethical, social, and political views.

Primal-scene memories of witnessing parental intercourse emerged in Sally's analysis. At three years of age, when she woke up screaming with nightmares, her mother, to quiet her, had her sleep the rest of the night in the parental bed, where Sally overheard the heavy breathing of intercourse. She fantasied that it was an attack by her father on her mother. She also witnessed parental intercourse at four and six years of age. There were no operable locks on the doors in the Rs home, and parental nudity and toilet behavior were also frequently observed by Sally, who became inhibited and afraid of boys.

Therapy: As with all anorexics, many different conflicts were displaced onto and masked by Sally's anorexic symptoms. Therapy focused on showing Sally the nature of her overstrict conscience, which demanded perfect behavior in herself and others. She was also hypercritical of her analyst. Memories and dreams revealed that she had developed this attitude by identifying with her mother's perfectionist attitudes.

Both Mr. and Mrs. R were referred for psychotherapy. Mrs. R came to understand that she was treating Sally very differently than Robert and that she had been pressuring her daughter to carry out certain of her own unfulfilled aspirations in life. The Rs moderated their overconcern with dieting and weight loss, and learned to tolerate and understand the emerging rebellious, critical adolescent behavior that Sally manifested as her anorexic symptoms subsided. Mrs. R changed her intrusive, controlling attitude toward her daughter. The parents also took some vacations together (alone) for the first time and began to permit themselves to quarrel in front of their children. Operable bedroom and bathroom locks were installed, and Sally was given a degree of privacy appropriate to her age.

C. Philip Wilson, 1983b
p. 36

Explaining to Parents

W E TAKE TIME TO tell parents about our philosophy of treatment. We explain that ours is a long-term psychodynamic approach aimed not only at alleviating the presenting symptoms but also at achieving lasting change in the underlying personality issues that helped to create the problem originally. We take care to share with the parents our feeling that no one is to blame in the situation and that their daughter's problem reflects not only her own difficulty but also a problem in the way the family as a whole is functioning. We suggest to the parents that their daughter's recovery depends on their learning to deal with the very difficult issues that arise when an anorectic or bulimic problem exists within a family. We tell parents that our goal is to help them to support growth and development in their child, through an increased understanding of their child and of themselves.

April Benson and Linda Futterman, 1985
p. 160

ㄹ

Family Therapy Is Not Sufficient if the Illness Has Existed for Any Length of Time

IN PATIENTS YOUNGER than fifteen or sixteen, family therapy seems to be an effective way of resolving problems. However, family therapy is not a sufficient treatment after the illness has existed for any length of time or when the patient is old enough to leave home. In these cases, while the family needs to gain an understanding of its own role in the development of the anorexic child, the patient needs individual help to develop the tools for leading a self-respecting individual life with a capacity for enjoyment and self-directed identity.

Hilde Bruch, 1988
p. 7

ㄹ

In Some Families the Patient Is Both Victim and Heroine

PARENTS PROJECT the unwanted parts of themselves into their child, then identify with those parts as extensions of the self. They perceive her, and she experiences herself, as greedy, demanding, incompetent, selfish, weak, dishonest, lazy, promiscuous, and so on. Through the projective identification, the parents and siblings are able to localize much of their warded-off anxiety and rage within her; they thereby maintain their own psychological equilibrium, and the stability of the family as a whole. The daughter accepts or identifies with these projections because she fears abandonment or rejection, and also because she is needed to fulfill a critical function for her family. For example, a father may unconsciously encourage and enjoy his daughter's acting out, but condemn her outwardly at the same time. A mother may be able to feel a kind of control over her own overwhelming feelings and needs by projecting them into the daughter, but remaining in close contact with her. Given this understanding of families with eating disorders, the bulimic or anorexic daughter emerges as both the victim and the heroine of the family. Effective treatment should incorporate a thorough appreciation of both these aspects of her identity, and her vital role in the stability of the family.

Laura Lynn Humphrey, 1991
p. 327

Unrealistic Family Expectations

MOST FAMILIES have unrealistic expectations—often reflecting their perfectionist ideal—with regard to the bulimia. They expect their child to stop bingeing all at once, which is impossible and often also undesirable.

Johan Vanderlinden, Ian Norre, and Walter Vandereycken, 1992
p. 146

11

Father–Daughter Relationship

Fathers Are Too Passive

ONE OF THE MAIN characteristics described by bulimics was the erratic behavior of their mothers, which unfortunately, was not modified by fathers, who were physically or emotionally absent, and too passive to intervene. Mothers were described as having had frequent rages, temper tantrums, and had great difficulty in regulating their own self-esteem. Perhaps worst of all, the mothers of bulimics were unpredictable. Overall, bulimics described themselves as never knowing what was right, what was wrong, what was punishable, what would go unnoticed, what was enough, or what was too much, all attitudes relating to the volatile inconsistencies of their mothers.

Deborah Brenner, 1983
p. 85

Fathers Are More Comfortable with a "Little Girl"

BOTH BETTY AND Claudia verbalized the typical anorexic fantasy (and probable fact) that they could relate to their fathers more directly in the prepubertal period than after adolescence. They felt that their fathers had been more comfortable with a "little girl."

Charles C. Hogan, 1983a
p. 126

ᄅ

Beneath a Facade of Hypermasculinity, Fathers Were Boyish, Dependent, and Unreliable

THE FATHERS WERE either superficially ultramasculine or were admired for their strength of character and their achievements. Many liked a poker game with the boys, spouted locker-room humor, enjoyed physical activities, and often spoke of women as sexual objects. Others were highly successful in professions that were exclusively male dominated and chose to spend most of their time away from home. Beneath this facade, these men were boyish, dependent, and unreliable, demanding nurturance and attention from their wives. While often successful in business or in professions, they were relegated to a childlike status at home with their wives essentially making all the decisions and taking on most responsibilities.

Jules Bemporad and John Ratey, 1985
p. 456

ᄅ

While Maintaining a Facade of Being Supportive, They Emotionally Abandoned Their Daughters

THE FATHERS WERE full of "empty promises" both of an explicit and implicit nature and continually disappointed their daughters. This is perhaps best epitomized by a comment of a recovered anorexic who recalled that when she felt really depressed in college, she could call her father who immediately understood how she felt by the tone of her voice but would do little more than offer sympathy or she could call her mother who could not appreciate her distress but would come up with a plan of action. The unreliability and dependency of the fathers of anorexic patients have not been particularly emphasized in the literature. Yet, we have found that the fathers would characteristically abandon, both in an emotional and at times in a physical way, the anorexic patient while maintaining the facade of being caring and supportive.

Jules Bemporad and John Ratey, 1985
p. 456

己

Many Confide that They Had Been Molested by Their Fathers in Childhood

THE FATHERS WERE remembered as almost polar opposites of the mothers. Patients described them as warm, emotional but also as unreliable and ultimately dangerous because of their uncontrollable sexual urges. In regard to this latter characteristic, many former anorexics confided that they believed they had been molested by their father in childhood although they could not remember any such occurrence. The sexual dreams of these women were all brutal and sadistic.

Jules Bemporad and John Ratey, 1985
p. 462

己

The Anorexic Adolescent Often Recalls Having Been Daddy's Favorite

PRECOCITY IN LITTLE girls is rarely limited to the premature development of intellectual and social skills. It also involves a pseudosexual advancement during their oedipal years. The anorexic adolescent consistently recalls having been Daddy's favorite: memories of greeting father at the door (to the exclusion of mother); attending business dinners and other important social engagements as Daddy's date; cooking dinner and breakfast for him while mother sleeps. More important, the anorexic patient usually remembers her special connectedness with father, a relationship in which both acknowledged nonverbally the father's preference for his daughter in the context of their unwitting exclusion of mother.

Here we observe the integration of two developmental facts. First, the lack of mirroring by the mother vitiates the normal integration of exhibitionistic and grandiose fantasies; thus the secret oedipal wish, the grandiose fantasy that father and daughter have an exclusive relationship which obviates mother's role, remains a psychologic actuality not subject to normal disappointment. Second, because the father at this stage of development fosters a uniquely exclusive relationship with his daughter, he provides (in an overstimulating manner) that echoing and mirroring for which the anorexic girl yearns. While not contributing to the progressive resolution of oedipal conflicts, he does help his daughter build compensatory narcissistic structures which would otherwise be missing. (It has been my experience that where fathers are unable to accomplish this task, we see borderline rather than narcissistic pathology).

Richard Geist, 1985
p. 274

The Father Exerts Strict Controls — Perhaps to Control Himself Indirectly

ANOTHER STRIKING aspect of the father–daughter relationship is that frequently they are much closer before adolescence begins. The bulimics will report poignant memories of the last time their father hugged them or complimented them, years earlier. Thus, the transition from "Daddy's little girl" to adolescent sexuality and separation is perhaps traumatic for them both. It may be that the fathers are alarmed by their own feelings and impulses in response to their daughters' sexual and emotional development. The daughter may even closely resemble his wife early in their relationship. Since the father himself has difficulty regulating his own tensions and impulses, he may respond to his daughter by abruptly and anxiously withdrawing his emotional closeness along with physical contact. This may also be related to why fathers exert such strict controls and standards over their daughters— that is, to control themselves indirectly.

Laura Lynn Humphrey, 1986
p. 328

A Secretive, Eroticized Relationship with the Father

EATING-DISORDER patients report having grown up in a family where they frequently experienced themselves as the mothering adult. Such precocity, which included the premature development of social and intellectual skills, is also remembered as including a secretive, eroticized relationship with the father during the girl's oedipal years and thereafter. In the role of mother of the house these girls recall a special connectedness with father in two specific ways: (1) as a relationship in which both acknowledged, usually nonverbally, the father's preference for his daughter in the context of their unwitting exclusion of the mother; and (2) as a relationship in which the girl experienced a basic feeling of her father's sustaining presence.

Richard Geist, 1989
p. 19

The Father's Entitlement Confirms the Impression that Dependence on a Man Means Subjugation to Him

JUST AS THE mother's behavior is a distortion of feminine relatedness, the father's behavior is a distortion and exaggeration of masculine strength into narcissistic isolation, autocracy, and misogyny. The father's entitlement confirms and underscores the child's impression that dependence on a man means subjugation to him, that there is much to be avoided and dreaded in the world of men.

Christopher Gordon, Eugene Beresin, and David Herzog, 1989
p. 38

⊒

Fathers Are Passive and Emotionally Unavailable

T HE FATHERS OF anorectic girls are usually fiercely ambitious in their professional roles and astonishingly passive and emotionally unavailable at home: "Oh, you better ask my wife about that. She takes care of feelings." These fathers expect polished performances from their children and wives but are content to let their wives rule the roost and dominate the trivialities of emotions and to mop up the untidinesses of the nursery. There is no sign anywhere of a desire between the parents.

Louise Kaplan, 1991
p. 463

12

Group Therapy

**Group Members Find It Hard to Express Disappointment
in or Hostility toward the Therapist**

Bulimic patients experience their symptom passively, as something which happens to them and over which they are powerless. There is a corresponding passivity in the transference to the therapist: there is a strong wish that therapy will provide a key or solution through which they will regain control. This makes the therapy difficult for most bulimic patients because, while they struggle to be "good patients," they feel increasingly frustrated that they are not being cured—that somehow they are not "getting it." They most frequently conceal this disappointment or show it in depressive actions such as missed meetings, becoming silent, or dropping out of the group. Early on in the group meetings, it is particularly difficult for the group to express disappointment in or hostility towards the therapist. . . . In every instance where I have been able to interview the patient after the termination, the patient has felt the group was probably worthwhile, but that she could probably not be helped there. Not one of these prematurely terminating patients could acknowledge directly her anger and disappointment with the group or with the therapist, although it seemed clearly present in every case.

W. Nicholson Browning, 1985
p. 146

Group Therapy for Anorexics Can Be Difficult

CERTAIN ASSUMPTIONS about anorexics in groups have been held up as reasons for not using group therapy. This may have more to do with poor selection of patients and inappropriate therapeutic techniques than with group therapy *per se*. The patients are likely to be silent, or preoccupied so much with food that this may be the sole topic of discussion; in fact, they may launch headlong into a competition to be the thinnest group member. Such disastrous results can be avoided with proper patient selection, appropriate therapeutic approach, and a therapist who is confident, experienced, and well supported. Nevertheless, the difficulties even for the most experienced therapist cannot be minimized. This form of therapy may be one of the most demanding and anxiety-provoking and least rewarding of the psychotherapies in general, and of those treatments currently in use for anorexia nervosa in particular. When it is successful, however, I believe it can offer the patient the opportunity for lasting change in social relationships, increased self-awareness, and ability to cope with emotions in a way that acts protectively against relapse, as individual therapy alone may fail to do.

Alyson Hall, 1985
p. 214

Withdrawal, Denial, and Intellectualization with a Group of Restrictors

A GROUP OF RESTRICTORS would be an enormous challenge for any therapist, as they are even less able to identify and express their feelings (particularly depression and anxiety) than bulimics, and, unless they have responded to previous treatment, will show more withdrawal, denial, and intellectualization.

Alyson Hall, 1985
p. 221

Wounds to Self-Esteem May Become Emotionally Bearable in a Group

THE THERAPIST'S empathic, nonjudgmental but interested stance encourages the individual to understand the meaning, for example, of increased vomiting, dieting, or a sudden wish to leave the group. Gradually this replaces the denial, repression, and acting out behavior with which many of our group members have previously coped with such experiences.

In this type of atmosphere, group members are able to experience wounds to self-esteem as emotionally bearable, often for the first time in memory. They are then able to make use of the opportunity to use the group experience to build the internal structure. This makes it possible to change repetitive and self-destructive behavior.

Diane Barth and Victoria Wurman, 1986
p. 739

In the Group Setting the Patients May Become Less Critical of Themselves

BEING "UNDERSTOOD" is a vital issue for these women, many of whom have never felt "really understood" by anyone in their lives. Our group members have often said that they feel understood by other group members because of the commonality of the experience. They also feel understood by the therapist, who models a style of nonjudgmental questioning with the intention of understanding. They begin to identify with the therapist's style and attempt to comprehend the meaning of their own and other group members' communications and feelings rather than to criticize themselves and others, as they are often wont to do. As one woman put it, "somehow just being in this group listening to you [the therapist] — your way of looking at this [the bulimic symptoms] like it has a meaning instead of like it's just *bad* — I'm becoming less critical . . . of myself, of others. . . ."

Diane Barth and Victoria Wurman, 1986
p. 743

〓

Help in Assertion, Focusing on One's Own Responsibility, and Maintaining a Balance between Self and Others

W HEN FAMILY therapy is not possible, group therapy (as well as support groups such as Overeaters Anonymous, Alcoholics Anonymous, and Al-Anon) can provide a forum for an individual to assert himself or herself, to set limits, to keep the focus on his or her own responsibility in an interaction, and to maintain a balance between self and others. This latter therapeutic task has as its goal not attaining autonomy in an exaggerated pseudo-self-sufficient sense, but rather attaining a better balance between one's relationship to oneself and one's relationships with others.

Deborah Brenner-Liss, 1986
p. 215

〓

Some Patients Find a Group Setting Safer than Individual Psychotherapy

A FEW SUBJECTS felt safer in a group setting, finding it easier to identify feelings and use the support of the group to own them without guilt, fear, or shame. This was particularly true for subjects who were developmentally arrested before consolidating trust. These subjects, unable to integrate their own hostility and aggression utilized splitting, projection, and projective identification as core defenses. Such individuals with borderline traits were plagued by omnipotent, magical thinking, terrified of the destructive power of their rage, threatened by its projection out into the world, and were ridden by unmodulated, primitive guilt. Although these women felt unworthy taking up the group's time, they found it safer than individual psychotherapy.

Eugene Beresin, Christopher Gordon, and David Herzog, 1989
p. 116

ᗺ

Bulimics Are Good at Detecting What Others Want and Providing It, So a Group May Appear to Be Functioning

THE SOCIAL AND ego deficits that make group desirable from the therapist's standpoint are the very reasons patients find group difficult. Compulsive eaters and bulimics struggle in group because of their social ineffectiveness, denial and somatization, ambivalence about changing eating patterns, and fear of being known. . . . An *effective* bulimia group is extraordinarily difficult to run. Bulimics are good at detecting what others want and providing it, so a group may appear to be functioning. But this appearance merely recapitulates one of members' original problems — a tendency to comply with others' expectations.

Linda Riebel, 1990
p. 404

ᗺ

Suggestions for Taking Care of the Therapist

GROUPS EXACT high costs from leaders, who must juggle many conflicting needs, and struggle to ensure group consistency in the face of the "no-shows" typical of eating disorder groups. The difficulty of managing the simplest level of group — the very presence of its members — can wear out the leader and provoke countertransference. Some practical suggestions for nurturing leaders are: Have a co-leader or someone to whom to vent; obtain consultation; realize dropouts are common in this population; evaluate carefully whether you really want to do groups; lead another group with a different population that provides a sense of leader satisfaction; take periodic vacations from leading groups.

Linda Riebel, 1990
p. 410

ㄹ

Group Therapy Can Counter the Isolation Characteristic of Eating Disorders

GROUP THERAPY provides eating-disordered patients with a safe environment to disclose and discuss their illness, which is usually a well-guarded secret shrouded in shame, guilt, and self-hatred. The isolation that develops around this disorder can be profound. Bulimic patients often have symptoms for 5–8 years before presenting for help. A psychodynamic group helps patients explore their inner experiences and their interpersonal relationships in the group, which acts as a paradigm for relationships in the outside world.

Helen Riess and J. Scott Rutan, 1992
p. 80

ㄹ

Psychodynamic Groups Are Difficult to Study and to Write About

IF PSYCHODYNAMICALLY oriented group psychotherapy is, in fact, a powerful and useful tool in the recovery from eating disorders, why is relatively little written on the subject, especially in comparison to time-limited treatments? There are many practical considerations that make psychodynamic groups more difficult to study and hence to write about. They are often of long duration and do not lend themselves to quick research studies. Because it is the process that promotes the cure, it is difficult to base progress on a measurable factor such as exposure to education or behavioral techniques that are used in time-limited treatments. Open-ended groups may last for years, during which individual therapy, pharmacotherapy, behavioral therapy, and cognitive therapy may have all played a part, making it difficult to conclude that it was psychodynamic group therapy alone that made a difference.

Helen Riess and J. Scott Rutan, 1992
p. 80

己

Some Patients Want a Quick Cure, Others Appreciate the Underlying Complexities

W ORTHY OF SPECULATION is whether there are in fact two separate populations of patients presenting with eating disorders: one group that is symptom focused, wanting a quick cure, and the other which appreciates that there are underlying psychological complexities for which eating symptoms provide temporary relief. Certainly not all patients who participate in time-limited treatment are ready for or interested in open-ended treatment at the end of the short-term group. One possibility is that we see patients at different stages in their illness. A patient who is convinced that all of her problems would be solved if she stopped binge-eating and purging at one stage in her illness may be the same patient who is ready to explore the meaning of her symptoms some years later. Whatever the mechanism that makes some patients able to make use of psychodynamic group treatment, it is important to identify the "readiness" of such individuals before recommending open-ended treatment.

Helen Riess and J. Scott Rutan, 1992
p. 82

己

Time-limited Treatment Can Be Used as a Preliminary Modality

B EHAVIORAL STRATEGIES such as goal setting, meal planning, food diaries, and planning activities that are incompatible with binge eating are all valuable tools that may give the patient a greater sense of control. Certainly there are some patients who are so deeply entrenched in their symptoms that insight into the underlying problems is impossible before the behaviors are brought under some degree of control. Thus, time-limited groups may be an entrance into treatment for the new patient, an adjunct to individual therapy, and/or an introduction to open-ended group therapy. Rather than regarding the different types of group treatments as mutually exclusive or incompatible, the authors suggest that using time-limited treatment as a preliminary modality before recommending open-ended group therapy can set the necessary framework for making the intensive experience of psychodynamic group therapy possible for this very challenging and multifaceted disorder.

Helen Riess and J. Scott Rutan, 1992
p. 83

13

Hospitalization

The Struggle with the Internalized Mother Goes On

Those who practice physical separation, that is, removing the patient from the family without providing psychoanalytic therapy for the patient, do not realize or do not accept the fact that the anorexia patient is dealing also with internalized objects and conflicts and that the struggle with the internalized mother will go on no matter where the patient is.

Melitta Sperling, 1955
p. 132

A Manipulative Approach Reconfirms the Anorexic's Earlier Experiences

As with drug treatments, refeeding through nursing care or behavioral manipulation (e.g., confining the half-resistant patient to bed and rewarding weight gain with greater freedom) apart from its humanly degrading aspects, may lead eventually to a deterioration of the condition in relation to that which would otherwise have naturally occurred. By adopting a stark mechanistic and manipulative approach one is often merely reconfirming for the anorectic her earlier experiences of life.

Arthur H. Crisp, 1980
p. 97

己

The Compulsory Patient Must Be Helped to Become a Voluntary Patient

THE ANORECTIC may quite clearly be in a state of terminal existential despair or she may be bland, hostile and denying any suicidal intent. Compulsory detention and care can often be seen within routine psychiatric practice as within acceptable limits under such circumstances. However, one can rarely hope to achieve anything other than a temporary amelioration of the crisis by such a step. The *compulsory* patient has got to be helped to become a *voluntary* patient at the very earliest opportunity if some greater impact on the course of events is sought.

Arthur H. Crisp, 1980
p. 149

己

Avoid Coercion

MEDICAL CARE BY the internist or pediatrician should be directed toward correcting the emergency situation that prompted patients' hospitalization. Toward that end, accurate weekly weighings, some awareness on the part of the nursing staff about how patients eat, and intravenous supplementary feedings and fluids may be indicated. These procedures can be accomplished, however, without attempts to coerce patients to eat or to put on weight. Any sense of desperate concern and worry over patients' condition is ill-advised and very counterproductive. Patients unconsciously view such concern as the consequence of their ability to control the staff through illness. Thus, their urge to stay sick or to get worse will increase, since control over the staff is unconsciously more important than getting better. A hard-hearted, indifferent, cold, or rejecting attitude toward patients is *not* advocated: all patients have the right to medical care by a thoughtful, considerate, and sensitive hospital staff. However, patients must recognize that the doctors and nurses are quite capable of dealing calmly with the situation, without conveying any sense of undue apprehension or panic. As most of the hospital care is performed by members of the nursing staff, their attitudes, behavior, and actual nursing care are of great importance in facilitating patients' recovery.

Ira Mintz, 1983a
p. 319

⊒

The Staff Should Be Aware of Patients' Fear of Being Controlled

IT IS IMPERATIVE that patients realize that the staff is available to help them, rather than to control them. A great deal of these patients' life experiences has left them feeling quite the opposite: that people are out to control them. In the hospital among a group of strangers, they feel even more helpless and vulnerable to the demands of others. The staff should recognize and be aware of patients' fear of being controlled and not do or say anything to increase it. Patients will fear and complain about being controlled even when no attempt has been made to control them. It can be pointed out that the hospital staff is available to be helpful and not to order them about or make all their decisions. In individual conversations with patients and in group meetings, the staff members should encourage patients to express their own ideas and to consider various alternative solutions; they should not fall into the attitude of "helpfully" providing solutions for patients. Patients often approach a staff member and ask what they should do. The staff member should be adroit enough to encourage patients to figure it out without making them feel rejected or antagonized. Infantile needs to be helpless, to be told what to do, and to be controlled take over and tend to preclude independent reasoning. The hospital staff should not unwittingly reinforce these regressed behavior patterns.

Ira Mintz, 1983a
p. 322

Provocative, Antagonistic Behavior May Reflect the Beginning of an Intrapsychic Shift

ANOTHER MANIFESTATION of this self-destructiveness takes the form of uncooperative, provocative, and antagonistic behavior. To provoke and frustrate the very people whose job it is to help when one is sick, hospitalized, and separated from friends and family, and realistically subject to the rules of the hospital staff, is truly a self-destructive act. If staff members are not well trained and alert to the possibility of this type of behavior, they may respond consciously or unconsciously with retaliatory actions. Or, equally inadvisable, they may feel unduly frustrated and give up trying to help patients at a crucial time. The provocative, antagonistic behavior may reflect the beginning of an intrapsychic shift from the anorexia to difficult behavior patterns; if so, it should be recognized and accepted as such, and considered in a potentially positive light, rather than with despair.

Ira Mintz, 1983a
p. 323

The Staff Needs to Be Able to Tolerate and Absorb Patients' Aggression

CHARACTERISTICALLY, these patients have always had difficulty in being reasonably and firmly assertive, in standing up for their rights, and in tolerating other people's anger and criticism. The aggressive drive can take the form of unruly, uncooperative, surly, and procrastinating behavior. This behavior is in marked contrast to previous behavior, which characteristically was cooperative, obedient, and submissive. In addition to recognizing that this type of change can be positive and that these "difficult" patients are beginning to deal with their conflicts over aggression, the staff needs to be able to tolerate and absorb patients' aggression without feeling threatened or defensive, without attempting to minimize the seriousness of their feelings, and without retaliating. It is of tremendous help to patients to realize that they can express feelings of anger without being punished, ignored, or abandoned. It increases their self-esteem, improves the quality of their relations with people, accentuates the value of verbal communication, improves mastery, and aids sublimations.

Ira Mintz, 1983a
p. 323

Coercion Is Likely to Be Only Temporarily Helpful

PATIENTS WHO are in danger of dying require hospitalization and treatment by the pediatrician or internist to help them recover from this emergency, but once they are out of medical danger, treatment should focus primarily on problems and conflicts, not eating. Anorexic patients are experts in dealing with coercion, and there are few therapists that have the ability to outdo them. Forcing patients to eat on Sunday frequently is followed by their starvation or vomiting on Monday. Treatment methods that coerce patients to eat are often temporarily successful. While they are in the hospital and under considerable pressure from a very controlled and controlling environment, they may eat. Once discharged, however, they starve themselves and lose all the weight they have gained.

Ira Mintz, 1983c
p. 98

Separation Unmasks Parental Overinvolvement and Extreme Boundness with the Identified Patient

SEPARATION QUICKLY provokes a dynamic instability within the family as a whole, bringing to light clues about the system's overall rigidity, and thus opening up potential therapeutic angles. To the extent that the patient has been the center of a peculiarly intense parental awareness, her sudden absence creates an unanticipated disruption of the family's usual homeostatic pattern. In this light, the functional role of the patient and her symptomatic behavior can be more readily discerned; the family's capacities for reorganization and change can be tested; and reasons for immobility and resistance to change can be identified. With most families, the separation brings to light previously denied patterns of overinvolvement and enmeshment, as parents voice doubt about their child's well-being and question the adequacy of care provided by the hospital staff. As these are exposed and discussed by the therapist, parents come to acknowledge, albeit with great reluctance, major rifts between them on approaches to child rearing. In other cases, separation triggers significant depression in one or more family members and in the patient as well, who expresses anguish at the grief and loneliness of the relative who, she believes, suffers most by her absence. This pattern is especially common in families where an absence of belonging and togetherness has been masked by over-involvement or extreme boundness with the identified patient.

Michael Strober and Joel Yager, 1984
p. 386

Challenging Staff and Overstepping Rules May Be Signs of Increased Sense of Identity and Growing Self-Esteem

THE RATE OF change among patients is highly variable. But in the majority of patients, behavior becomes more decidedly "adolescent"—

humorous, provocative, and sometimes sexual. The patients may take risks to challenge staff and overstep rules (e.g., use of foul language); these are signs of an incipient sense of identity and mastery and a more internalized self-esteem. Although the patient is not complimented or reinforced for these changes, they are nurtured by the staff's own challenging and teasing responses and the setting of limits on grossly disruptive behavior. Many patients report that this is the first time they have dared to be boisterous or defiant, and that they feel good about not being approached as though they were too fragile to manage confrontation.

Michael Strober and Joel Yager, 1984
p. 388

己

Weight Gain Alone Should Not Determine When the Patient Can Safely Leave the Hospital

W HERE NARCISSISTIC rage continues to exist and where the self remains fragmented, there is an ongoing risk of suicide; not active attempts to kill oneself, but passive diffidence to life whenever the connection to the narcissistically perceived environment is disrupted. In this context, any attempts to determine when a patient may safely leave the hospital should never depend on weight gain. Rather we must ask: (1) whether weight has been stabilized at a medically safe level; (2) whether a selfobject transference has been established with the therapist; and (3) whether there are clear indications that soothing mechanisms are becoming internalized. A positive response to these three questions suggests that the rekindling of dormant elements of the self has commenced and the patient is becoming capable of caring for herself.

Richard Geist, 1985
p. 284

己

After Discharge, Groups Can Provide Auxiliary
Ego Support

EVEN IN AN OUTPATIENT context, additional structure may need to be provided by the environment. If the individual is out of the hospital but not able to work or go to school, a daytime hospital program could help her to maintain herself in better equilibrium between individual therapy sessions. Even for those clients who are functioning well enough to work or attend school, free (unstructured) time on evenings and weekends is often disorganizing enough that it triggers episodes of bingeing and vomiting. The additional support of a bulimic group or other support networks such as Overeaters Anonymous may be crucial. Internalized self-regulatory capacities need to be developed in a context of "good enough care" and in conjunction with caring, involved people available to offer auxiliary ego support and soothing. Only in such a context can the recovering bulimic begin to allow bodily and emotional sensations to be felt, get help managing and identifying them, and begin to learn better ways of maintaining equilibrium despite external or internal problems.

Deborah Brenner-Liss, 1986
p. 213

The Hospital Program Needs to Provide Aspects of the
Early Holding Environment

MY COLLEAGUES and I, working from a developmental object relations model, proposed that the hospital refeeding program for anorexics functions as a therapeutic holding environment with many of the characteristics of Winnicott's mother–infant holding environment. The severely ill anorexic patient is assumed to be at a regressed level of ego function and to have developmental deficits stemming from parenting failures in the separation-individuation period of infant development. We suggested that the hospital program needs to provide those elements of the early holding environment that tend to be missing in these patients' families, the crucial functions being *protective structure, empathic availability, support of individuation, reliability,* and *tolerance for regression.* It was recommended that the medical and nursing staff responsible for administering the refeeding program be familiar with these principles in order to better manage the patients and to avoid the negative countertransference reactions that the patients and their families often provoke.

Steven Stern, 1986
p. 235

□

Avoid the Dangers of Both Overcontrol and Undercontrol

T HE ANOREXIC patient is making prominent from the outset perhaps her most fundamental unsolved developmental problem: obtaining *appropriate* parental control, i.e., control that is in *her* interests and takes into account *her* needs. In responding to tests of this nature, a number of general principles seem applicable, given what we know about the early traumas in this domain:

1. Keep the patient's needs and interests primary at all times.
2. Try to provide only as much structure or control as the patient really needs and only in those areas where she needs it.
3. Take a clear, firm, therapeutic stand once you have made your assessment. State your reasons for taking it, but *don't* insist that the patient agree with you or even, initially, comply. However, equally importantly,
4. Set clear behavioral limits and don't let the patient violate these within your system.
5. Continue to reassess the needs for control over time, as treatment progresses.

Applying these principles to the evaluator's dilemma described above, the principle task is to determine how much external structure the patient needs to protect her from the dangers of her self-destructive eating behavior while simultaneously respecting her need for autonomy and self-control. Thus, unless there is an acute medical crisis, it is usually advisable to give the patient the benefit of the doubt and permit an initial course of outpatient treatment *with the understanding* that if she cannot start gaining weight, or at least stop losing, hospitalization will again have to be considered. This kind of approach avoids both the dangers of overcontrol and undercontrol.

Steven Stern, 1986
p. 240

◲

Responding to the Patient's Tests

THE PATIENT has an unconscious concern that the treatment setting will simply impose its own needs and expectations in much the same way that the family has. Thus, many patients will test the treatment environment, unconsciously attempting to provoke just such a response. The major transference tests seem to be of three types:

1. Tests in which the staff are provoked to *curtail the patient's autonomy via overcontrol* (usually because the patient has acted out or expressed her independence in a self-destructive way).
2. Tests in which the patient expresses her autonomy in such a way as to provoke *retaliation or abandonment* (usually by being provocatively noncompliant, demanding, complaining, rejecting, or otherwise unpleasant).
3. Tests in which the therapist or staff are provoked to *push the patient too quickly to assert her own needs and feelings*, not appreciating the adaptive value of her self-denial in the family and within her own ego ideal. (This kind of countertransference occurs in response to the patient's extreme denial, overcompliance, or seemingly self-destructive collusion with familial expectations.)

Experience suggests that in responding to tests of this nature it is helpful to apply a number of general principles and assumptions:

1. Create conditions in which separation and individuation are encouraged and facilitated but not demanded or forced.
2. Neither collude with, nor overreact to, the patient's self-destructive ways of expressing autonomy.
3. Appreciate the adaptive value of the patient's self-sacrificing stance and the risks that she feels may be involved both for herself and her family in giving this up.
4. Assume that individuation and self-assertion are natural human tendencies and will almost certainly reemerge spontaneously when the patient feels it is safe to allow them to do so.
5. In general, *do not need* the patient to behave in any particular way, including ways that may be deemed to be in her best interest. To do so deprives the patient of initiative at a process level.

Steven Stern, 1986
p. 243

Angry Feelings Surface Very Quickly
after Admission

WHEN MOST ANOREXIC and bulimic patients initially enter treatment they consciously deny angry feelings. The underlying rage is of course there, but it is managed with defenses such as splitting, projective identification, or turning the anger against the self, or it is discharged indirectly through the anorexic or bulimic symptoms. Bringing the patient into the hospital and controlling her symptoms obviously blocks the latter form of discharge. Thus, it is not unusual for angry feelings to surface very quickly after admission. Often these are expressed in complaints about the program and/or the staff. The more defensive modes of expressing anger – splitting, projection, manipulativeness, turning it inward—become evident as the patient engages with the milieu and develops relationships with the staff.

Steven Stern, 1986
p. 247

〓

The Displacement of Conflicts from the Interpersonal and Intrapsychic Fields to the Mind–Body Field

JUST AS THERE were innumerable opportunities to engage in the task of personalization and to note the blurring of psychological feeling states with body states, so there were innumerable opportunities to note the displacement of conflicts from the interpersonal and intrapsychic fields to the mind–body field. One day Sara came to an hour and commented on her exclusion from a clique of young women patients in the Inn. She said they mocked her, cut her down, and avoided her. She felt totally out of control, helpless, and hopeless, because she was not able to control them and make them stop the hurtful behavior vis-à-vis her. I asked what she had done to try to effect some change in her relationship with them. She said she had lost more weight. I said I was puzzled by that; how would that change her relationship with these women? She said, "Well, for example, I walked into the dining room to get a cup of coffee during dinner last night. These women were all sitting at a table with one another when I came in. They became obviously quiet when I passed them." Then she heard someone say something very nasty about her and the whole table erupted into laughter. I said, "Gee, that must have hurt your feelings. I think in that situation I would feel hurt, embarrassed, self-conscious, frustrated, sad, and very angry, with all those feelings mixed up with one another in some painful, complicated way. Is that how you felt?" She said, "No, I felt panic very fleetingly, and then I felt fat. So I left the dining room, vomited, exercised, and later that evening I took some laxatives, and after that I felt better." I said I was again puzzled. I could understand feeling better because of losing weight if the problem was being fat, but in this case the problem seemed to be feelings that got stirred up in her by hostile interactions with peers. I didn't think weight reduction would alter Sara's relationship with her peers. It seemed to me she would be better off sitting down with these women and talking with them about how they treated her, how that affected her, and asking them straightforwardly to stop being hurtful. If they weren't willing to do that, and she was not able to change them, then I thought she would be wise to try to change herself in the sense of changing her reaction to their hostilities so that she no longer felt fat when hurt by them, and therefore no longer engaged in activities that were hurtful to her body.

Sara said that she didn't think she would be able to do that on her own. I then suggested she bring it up in a combined patient–staff meeting and ask other patients and staff members what they had observed in her interactions with the members of this clique, to let them know how she experienced them, and ask them for some help with regard to this very problematic relationship. That she was willing to do, and when she did, she discovered that a number of patients and various staff members were quite supportive of her and were helpful to her with this clique. Their efforts led subsequently to much improved relationships between Sara and the members of the clique. Sara was very pleased when she was able to effect this change, and the good experience in the group led her to increase her participation in the group life of the hospital.

There were countless other opportunities to note occasions when Sara moved from an interpersonal interaction that stirred up feelings in her that she felt out of control of, and to note that rather than continuing to struggle either with the person, to change them, or with herself, to change herself in the sense of changing her reaction to that person, she instead shifted to the mind–body field. There she reassured herself that she was not in fact totally helpless and out of control of everything by redemonstrating to herself her control over her body's weight by again losing yet more weight. However, as the frequency of her success in the interpersonal arena increased, the frequency of the displacement of interpersonal and intrapsychic conflicts to the mind–body field slowly decreased.

James Sacksteder, 1989a
p. 416

14

Menstruation

Amenorrhea Often Precedes Weight Loss

THE EARLY ONSET of amenorrhea proves that anorexia nervosa is not a simple matter of undernourishment. The abrupt cessation of the menses, even before loss of appetite and weight are apparent, is the rule in a large number of cases.

Helmut Thomä, 1967
p. 30

Punished for Being Female and for Having Grown Up

I WAS HORRIFIED and disgusted by menstruation rather than by sexuality. I felt that some dreadful punishment had been visited upon me, punishment for a crime which I had never committed. But I think I knew unconsciously that the supposed crime was twofold: I was being punished for being female and for having grown up. At the same time I didn't *feel* female, in the sexual sense. Neither did I feel male, but rather neuter, as a child might feel itself to be neuter. And I certainly didn't feel grown-up. The crimes in question had been committed by my body, not by me.

Sheila MacLeod, 1982
p. 39

⊇

Wanting to Be a Little Girl

I DIDN'T WANT my periods to start again. That I had managed to stop them was a major achievement on my part. Instead of growing up, I had, as it were, grown down, and thus reversed a natural biological process. I was no longer a woman. I was what I wanted to be: a girl. I was what I felt unconsciously I had never had a chance to be: a little girl.

Sheila MacLeod, 1982
p. 67

⊇

Menstruation as Loss and Separation

MENSTRUATION CAN symbolize a sense of deprivation in human relationships. Depression over menstruation is often described as a reflection of disappointment at not being pregnant. In the more symbiotic type of woman, pregnancy can often internally symbolize, through identification with the fetus, the realization of the fantasy of symbiotic reunion of the child with the mother, and in this sense, menstruation can symbolize the disruption of such a fantasy and the unconscious realization and confrontation of the reality of separation from the mother. The bleeding can represent loss and separation, loss of a part of oneself, loss of the child in oneself, and separation from a childhood attachment to the mother.

Cecil Mushatt, 1982b
p. 261

⊇

Unwillingness to Accept Femininity

MENSTRUATION IS disturbed or absent in anorexia and stands for an unwillingness to accept femininity. Treatment goals should be directed toward correcting major intrapsychic conflict rather than just resolving its symptomatic consequences (e.g., not eating, not menstruating). Otherwise, the patient is left with major disabilities associated with her ability to enjoy her sexuality and feminine identity. In addition, her capacity to deal with pregnancy and motherhood will be impaired.

Ira Mintz, 1983e
p. 344

If Significant Unconscious Conflicts Are Unresolved, Amenorrhea Continues

W E HAVE FOUND that all the physical signs and symptoms of anorexia nervosa—hypothermia, lanugo hair, hypotension, bradycardia, anemia, and leukocytosis—return to normal when patients resume normal eating as a result of psychodynamic treatment. However, if significant unconscious conflicts have not been resolved, the menstrual cycle may not become normal even though the patient's weight returns to normal limits.

C. Philip Wilson, 1983a
p. 3

Fear of Invasion

T HE FEAR OF pregnancy must not be interpreted as a sexual fear but rather as a sexual symbol of a more frightening experience, namely that of being invaded and distended by the primary object, that is the mother.

Mara Selvini Palazzoli, 1988
p. 164

Menarche Returns Late in Treatment

A LATE-ADOLESCENT girl who had been a bulimic anorexic and virtually amenorrheic since early adolescence, came to treatment weighing about 80 pounds, with a severely cachectic appearance. She was both restricting her diet and bingeing and inducing vomiting four to five times daily. Insight which developed much later on in the therapy revealed that her relentless need to binge and purge was related to frustration and rage toward her controlling parents, who babied and coddled her. She had virtually no social activity with peers. In fact, she had been agoraphobic and she had been able to do little without being accompanied by her mother or some family member. Several months into treatment, her symptoms began to subside. Within a year or so, her life in almost all of its aspects approached the normal range, as she now had the teen-age friends and activities which had been bypassed in her earlier adolescence. However, it was not until three years into her therapy, when she had resolved certain of her sexual conflicts, that menarche came. . . . Terminating therapy when the patient appears to be physically healthy, but before menstruation has resumed, may be a foreshortening of treatment and a disservice to the patient.

Roberta Wennik-Kaplan, 1990
p. 5

15

Mother–Daughter Relationship

Killing the Mother in Her Own Body

T HE PATIENT WAS dominated by the idea that she must not want to eat, in order not to have the body of a woman, *not to become like her mother*, whom she hated and killed in her own body. . . . The prohibition against food is derived from the idea: "I do not want to have the body of a woman." This idea is the result of an instinctual conflict which arises from oral anxiety and oral hatred towards the mother, and by way of identification, rages against the subject's body, evoking a paranoid illness with a reversal of aggression against the self.

Therese Benedek, 1934
p. 48

Anorexia Is the Expression of a Struggle in the Very Early Period of the Patient's Attachment to Her Mother

I N THIS PATIENT this symptom complex seemed to indicate a serious disturbance. It was an expression of many conflicts besides those which referred to the sexual sphere — which some investigators maintain the outstanding or main symptom. There was a deeper struggle going on within the patient—a struggle involving not only fight and defense against sexual drives, but drives which were more diffuse and pertained to disturbances in the whole personality structure. These referred mainly to the very early period of the patient's attachment to her mother.

Sandor Lorand, 1943
p. 282

ᘝ

Conflicted Behavior towards Food Represents Conflicted Emotions towards the Mother

MUCH OF THE child's conflicting behavior towards food does not originate from loss of appetite or a lessened need to eat, etc., but from conflicting emotions towards the mother which are transferred on to the food which is a symbol for her. Ambivalence towards the mother may express itself as fluctuations between over-eating and refusal of food; guilty feelings towards the mother and a consequent inability to enjoy her affection as an inability to enjoy food; obstinacy and hostility towards the mother as a struggle against being fed.

Anna Freud, 1946
p. 126

ᘝ

The Patient Assumes Control over Her Own and Her Mother's Life

ANOREXICS USE food to reverse the early childhood situation when mother was in control of food and, by extension, the patient's life. By assuming control over food intake, the patient puts herself in the place of the mother and assumes control over her own and her mother's life. Some of these patients like to feed or overfeed others, especially their mothers, while not eating themselves. This makes the patient a better mother than her own mother.

Melitta Sperling, 1955
p. 75

⊒

The Mother Received Poor Maternal Care

T HE MOTHER OF the typical anorectic patient is an emotionally immature woman who feels that she received poor maternal care. She was, and continues to be, dependent upon her own mother, a controlling woman who provides criticism but little support, and who feels an obligation to direct her daughter's life.

Bertram J. Cohler, 1977
p. 356

⊒

The Mother of the Anorectic Is an Emotionally Immature Woman Who Often Continues to Be Dependent on Her Own Mother

T HE ANORECTIC'S mother is typically perfectionistic, domineering, overwhelming, overcaring, and obsessively opinionated about her child, to the extent that the girl, as a young adolescent, is unprepared for youth. The mother of the anorectic is an emotionally immature woman who often continues to be dependent on her own mother, also a controlling woman who can only criticize her daughter and try to control her life—and later, directly and indirectly—the life of her granddaughter.

John Sours, 1980
p. 6

⊒

There Are Clues of Impaired Mother–Infant Relations in the First Year of Life

W E NEED TO ASK whether the anorexic girl or the child with a vulnerability towards an eating disorder truly does not manifest severe enough symptoms until she is on the brink of death. The avalanche of research that has just begun on infancy and prevention work suggests that there are clues of impaired mother–infant relations in the first year of life. By using the early feeding relationship as a paradigm of mother–child interaction, we can hopefully integrate psychoanalytic theory with behavioral data in such a way that we gain greater access to primary prevention in the first six months of life.

Jan Charone, 1982
p. 39

⊐

Many of These Patients Are Aware of Their Mother's Demanding Infantile Needs

MANY OF THESE patients are well aware consciously of the demanding, infantile needs of the mother. One patient pointed out in an early session that her mother was a "bigger baby" than she was and would have "temper tantrums" when she didn't get what she wanted. Another patient observed that her mother was an "infant" who would withdraw into "depressions or nerves" when her needs were frustrated. A third patient was consciously aware of her mother's need for fusion, as the mother insisted that they knew each other "completely" and could "read each other's thoughts and feelings." While there is projective identification at work here, the descriptions of mother's activities and the quotations of mother's words indicate the validity of these patients' observations.

Charles C. Hogan, 1983b
p. 157

⊐

Regression Causes Infantile Ties to the Mother to Reemerge

THE PATIENT'S GUILT over unconscious feelings of aggression and sexuality is assuaged by a strict punishing conscience that dictates starvation, illness and the possibility of death, and the deprivation of all pleasurable foods. Regression causes the infantile ties to the mother, which never have been severed, to reemerge with an archaic, omnipotent ego that strives for megalomanic control over food, the patient's body, and, through them, the external world.

Ira Mintz, 1983c
p. 94

己

Mother's Emptiness

MARY RECOLLECTED sitting on Mother's knee, listening to a funny story on the radio. There had been no sign of happiness or pleasure on Mother's face. Mother never hugged or kissed her – she seemed to hide a secret sorrow. Like many of my patients Mary had studied the book entitled "The Scream." The cover picture was of an open mouth screaming. She felt that the scream and the hungry longing it depicted was "what Mother was about." She reflected "She wasn't a face, but just a mouth screaming for something to be put in." I suggested that this was perhaps what Mary felt about herself and if a mother is felt to be empty, the infant is compelled to suck her dry or to starve. It must be terrifying to feel so hungry and so very angry at the mother's emptiness.

Marjorie Sprince, 1984
p. 208

己

Chronic History of Unempathic Responses

PENNY, A 20-YEAR-OLD anorexic patient, recalled poignantly her adolescent attempts to dress up for special occasions – dates, academic affairs, and social gatherings. "It was hard to combine everything so it felt like me, and when I asked my mother how I looked she'd always find something wrong." Instead of the admiration, approval, and confirmation for which Penny yearned, her mother responded critically, isolating and negating a single element of her daughter's complete presence. "You'd look fine if it weren't for your hair; let me fix it," or "Yes, dear, you look nice, but that necklace ruins the whole thing. I'll get you another." Within the therapeutic space, patients relive a chronic history of such unempathic responses. In Penny's case her mother could not allow her daughter to weave makeup, jewelry, clothes, and hairstyle into a unique motif; rather, she splintered the synthesizing effort and then, in an attempt to reintegrate her daughter's wholeness, substituted a hairstyle and necklace of the mother's choosing. Only under this patchwork of imposed conditions could mother respond approvingly to the daughter she had "remade" in her own image.

Richard Geist, 1985
p. 272

⊒

Mothers of Infantile Anorexics Try to Impose
Their Will on the Infant

THE PRESENT STUDY examines the interactional patterns of mothers and infants who present with a separation disorder (infantile anorexia disorder). . . . These mothers lacked the flexibility to pace their behavior according to their infant's cues and instead, tried to impose their will on the infant. Feeding became a chore instead of an enjoyable growing experience through which the infant could establish increasing autonomy. The mothers of normally feeding infants were observed to wait more often for the infant to initiate interactions and to allow greater participation in the feeding. Another striking difference between the two groups of mothers was affective expression. Whereas the mothers in the control group appeared more cheerful and at ease, the mothers of the feeding disordered group appeared more sad, distressed, and/or angry. In general, the affect of the mothers and their infants in both groups appeared to mirror one another.

Irene Chatoor, James Egan, Pamela Getson,
Edgardo Menvielle, and Regina O'Donnell, 1987
p. 538

⊒

Separation-Individuation Is More Difficult for
Girls than for Boys

✝

IT IS NOW CLEAR that the process of separation-individuation from the pre-oedipal mother is enormously more difficult for girls than for boys, and that conflicts over separation-individuation persist much longer in females. The reasons for this can be outlined only briefly here, but many of them are clearly relevant to women's greater propensity to develop eating disorders in adolescence and early adulthood.

1. On the mother's side there is far more blurring of boundaries and identification with female than with male children. Mothers are less able to see daughters as distinctively different from themselves and tend thus to be more controlling and possessive with them.

2. It follows that mothers are also more heavily invested in daughters as narcissistic extensions of themselves, projecting on to them their own hopes, fears, and fantasies about femininity. They feel more threatened, and hence tend to be more manipulative and controlling, if the daughter falls short of these ideals, than they would be with a son.

3. If separation from the mother is more difficult for the daughter, individuation poses further problems. In the second year of life, during the crucial period of gender-identity formation, the girl must pull away from her mother and develop an individual identity distinct from hers, yet at the same time learn to identify with the mother as a female, i.e., become in essence the same as her. The boy can instead use identification with his father's masculinity to help him individuate from the mother, rather than being pulled back constantly into a merger with the symbiotic primary caretaker.

4. Physical differences may also contribute to the girl's difficulties in the rapprochement phase, with its push towards independence and self-control. Unlike the boy she has no external, easily handled genital that can be associated with intense physical sensations, and this may lead to much greater anxiety about

bodily intactness and loss of control. Such fears enhance her dependence on the mother and need for reassurance and support at the same time as she is trying to break away and establish self-mastery.

5. The rapprochement or anal phase is characterized in both sexes by a battle for the control of bodily functions, including feeding as well as elimination. Most observers agree that boys in this period are much more easily able to turn away and direct their aggressive energies to mastery of the outside world. Girls are more conflicted, being both more dependent on and identified with the mother, and fearful and angry at the mother's intrusiveness and control (both real and projected). The solution seems to be for the girl, out of fear and guilt over her own aggressive impulses, to identify with the mother's controlling and caretaking functions and thereby to inhibit her own sadism and aggression towards the mother and the outside world. She turns her aggressive energies inwards to self control, thereby becoming typically cleaner, neater, and more docile than the boy. The price paid, however, is strong repression of pregenital messiness and sexuality and a lifelong tendency to view the body guiltily as an enemy to be controlled rather than as a source of pleasure to be enjoyed.

6. This conflict, rooted in fear of and intense dependence on the mother, is further exacerbated during the oedipal phase with its jealous rivalry for the father's affections, when fear of the mother's retaliation may give the girl reason to be anxious about assuming the female sexual role and to reaffirm, not without hostile ambivalence, her dependence on the mother.

Hilary J. Beattie, 1988
p. 454

己

Unable to See Her Daughter as Separate

THE TYPICAL MOTHER of the anorexia nervosa patient is an aggressively overprotective and unresponsive woman, and as such incapable of considering her daughter as a person in her own right.

Mara Selvini Palazzoli, 1988
p. 159

⊒

There Is Both a Wish for a Soothing Maternal Object and a Fear of an Unresponsive Mother

WHEN THE DEFENSES have been worked through, it becomes apparent that they were at the service of obliterating the wish for closeness with a soothing maternal object that makes it all better. The wish has its counterbalance in the fear of an alternatively unresponsive or critical mother who tolerates only a perfect child and who is not able to make emotional contact with the actual child.

Ana-Maria Rizzuto, 1988
p. 372

⊒

The Sadomasochistic Features of the Mother–Daughter Relationship Are Dissociated and Repressed

PRIOR TO BECOMING anorexic, the psyche–soma split is usually not noticeable but a dissociation between a true self and a false self organization is. The false self organization, like the psyche–soma split, is an adaptation to a failure in the maternal provision of infant care. Intrusive, impinging, unattuned maternal care leads to both dissociations. The false self organization of the anorexic is marked by excessive compliance and dependence on the mother. As the false self develops it provides a facade of social conformity and achievement and masks ongoing failures in personalization, in separation-individuation, in self/selfobject development, and identity formation.

Both mother and daughter promote and enjoy an illusion of an ongoing good relationship with one another, free of all hostility. In fact, each idealizes the other and the relationship. Closer scrutiny of the relationship, however, reveals the persecutory and sadomasochistic features of the relationship that mother and daughter and other family members usually dissociate, split off, isolate, deny, project, and repress.

James Sacksteder, 1989b
p. 391

ㄹ

Differentiation without Having to Separate
Psychologically from the Mother

T HE DAUGHTER, THEN, is torn between the urgings of her own developmental strivings and her equally strong need to meet the narcissistic needs of the mother. In this context, the function of eating-disorder symptoms is to give her the sensation of differentiation without having to separate psychologically from the mother.

Susan H. Sands, 1989
p. 93

16

The Patient Speaks

Being Hungry Has the Same Effect as a Drug, and You Feel Outside Your Body

MY THOUGHT PROCESSES became very unrealistic. I felt I had to do something I didn't want to do for a higher purpose. That took over my life. It all went haywire. I created a new image for myself and disciplined myself to a new way of life. My body became the visual symbol of pure ascetic and aesthetics, of being sort of untouchable in terms of criticism. Everything became very intense and very intellectual, but absolutely untouchable. If you indulge in being a person who doesn't eat and who stays up all night, then you can't admit "I feel miserable" or "I feel hungry." Being hungry has the same effect as a drug, and you feel outside your body. You are truly beside yourself—and then you are in a different state of consciousness and you can undergo pain without reacting. That's what I did with hunger. I knew it was there—I can recall and bring it to my consciousness—but at that time I did not feel pain. It was like self-hypnosis. For a long time I couldn't talk about it because I was scared it would be taken away from me.

quoted by Hilde Bruch, 1978
p. 18

己

Anger

I CANNOT HELP feeling anger but I certainly can help showing it.

quoted by Hilde Bruch, 1982a
p. 8

己

The Body Is the Only Weapon in the
Bid for Autonomy

M<small>Y ONLY WEAPON</small> in my bid for autonomy was to go on strike. Withdrawal of labor, in the literal sense, would have been impractical and, more importantly, would have caused further destruction to my self-esteem in that without work (schoolwork) I should have had and have been less than the nothing I already felt myself to have and to be. So I "chose" a form of passive resistance. Just as the worker's ultimate weapon in his negotiation with management is his labor and the threat of its withdrawal, so my body was my ultimate and, to me, only, weapon in my bid for autonomy. It was the only thing I owned, the only thing which could not be taken away from me.

Sheila MacLeod, 1982
p. 56

己

Omnipotence

A<small>S MY WEIGHT</small> decreased, so did my helplessness. Anorexia provided me with the illusion that I was in control, not only of my body and my own status within the community, but of that community itself and, finally, of the biological processes which others around me were powerless to influence. In short, I became convinced of my own omnipotence. The conviction started from my body and the discovery that no one could prevent me—if I were determined enough—from treating it as I wished. I had discovered an area of my life over which others had no control.

Sheila MacLeod, 1982
p. 66

⊐

Fear of Sexuality

W HEN I WAS anorexic I had only dim feelings of resentment as to how my body was destined to be used, and the thought of anything as positive and specific as penetration never entered my mind. Incredible as it may seem, I never thought about sex at all, and didn't even masturbate: starvation reduces libido. However, I now see my very sexlessness as a flight from sexuality, and mainly *my own* sexuality. I think I was afraid that, once I recognized it, it too might get out of control—just like my body in general.

Sheila MacLeod, 1982
p. 68

⊐

"Look How Messed Up I Am"

"Let me show you how skinny I am. It's disgusting. [Pulling up her long sleeves] Look at my bones. I have to have something in my mouth all the time: gum, cigarettes, candy. I chew 20 sticks of gum a day. I don't eat regular food. . . . I stuff myself and then I vomit. I used to weigh 110, then I went down to 70. Now I'm up to 80. . . . I like to be with people constantly. You know, to have my feedings. . . . I'm happy when I'm told how skinny I am, that's how nuts I am.

"Look at this. [Here she pushed down her jeans to reveal a mass of scar tissue on her abdomen.] I get this from burning myself with the hot-water bottle when my stomach hurts and I'm constipated. . . . I can't stand it when I'm constipated. I have to get it out. I take laxatives every night, sometimes 50 or 60. . . . Then I stay up most of the night exercising or smoking to keep up my metabolism so that I don't put on any weight. . . . I do everything to extremes. When I vomit, I jam my fingers down my throat so hard. . . . [Here she revealed a series of long-standing scars on the dorsum of her fingers where the upper teeth had gashed the skin from the violence of her thrust into her mouth.]"

In her hyperactive, agitated state, she was almost oblivious to the analyst's presence and certainly was not attuned to his responses since thus far he had had almost no opportunity to make a comment. This was essentially the tenor of her early therapeutic contacts. She continued, "If someone doesn't call me, I get frustrated and act hysterical. . . . and then I go and eat the house up. . . . I have to always be in control. . . . When I get too frustrated, I get so depressed that I think of killing myself. . . . I can't be alone." She suddenly looked directly at the analyst, instead of talking to the air. "I feel that I'm not making contact with you. I really wanted to see someone else, you know, and because his office was in W – – – , he thought that it was too far. I was furious. I really liked Dr. L. [her previous analyst] very much."

The analyst asked her why her previous therapy had failed if she had liked that analyst so much. She reflected for a moment, one of the first pauses in her outpouring, and then replied, "I don't know. I was very upset when he said that he couldn't help me. . . . He was very honest though." The analyst asked her if she had felt a sense of triumph at his defeat. "No . . . well . . . I don't know. Can you help me?" The analyst replied that she was so self-destructive that she might try to wreck this treatment, too. "No, I won't do that again. . . . You're pretty smart, maybe I did do that." So ended the first interview.

Ira Mintz, 1983d
p. 219

Before Therapy I Was Upset about Food, but I Wasn't Unhappy about My Life

I WENT HOME Sunday night and started looking through old notebooks. I don't think I was unhappy before I started therapy, not as unhappy as I am now. That last year of college I wrote pages and pages about being upset about food. I even wrote that I wanted to die because of what was happening with food. But I wasn't unhappy about my life. Most days I wrote about how much I loved my family, and how wonderful my mother was and how wonderful my father was . . . It seems like I was so much healthier then! Now I'm always angry at my family, or feeling guilty about not calling them every day.

quoted by Deborah Brenner-Liss, 1986
p. 218

The Worst Loss

As a patient, Rita, put it: "I have never been left to experience things in my own way. This is the worst loss anyone can suffer. It leads to emptiness, to a lack of emotional contact with life, to a lack of real vitality, of whatever makes you feel yourself instead of a heavy, shapeless thing."

Mara Selvini Palazzoli, 1988
p. 159

I Got Angry through Anorexia Nervosa

Mother cloned me. I did what she wanted, when she wanted it and it made her so happy and it made me happy. "Oh, isn't she wonderful," said my mother all the time. I'm a victim, but I also got stroked unconditionally. As a teenager my mother told me what to want, what to wear, to wear this bra or that bra. She was very, very intrusive. I felt I couldn't control anything in my life. I confused nurturance and food. I couldn't get angry, because it would be like destroying someone else, like Mother. It felt like she would hate me forever. I got angry through anorexia nervosa. It was my last hope. It's my own body and this was my last ditch effort.

quoted by Eugene Beresin, Christopher Gordon, and
David Herzog, 1989
p. 111

日

Behavior Modification Is a Joke Because
Anorectics Are Too Smart

In some ways the hospital was valuable, providing a space to be sick, but it also defeated the root problems of anorexia, that is, the need to form a self, which is in self-control, aware of my needs and not controlled. I had been controlled all my life, which led to an inability to take care of myself. In the hospital, it was safe to eat, but I was totally aware that I could re-lose the weight when discharged. It focused on my illness and not a family problem. Behavior modification is a joke because anorectics are too smart. They do what they want to do and what they need to do to get out. No one can make you get better.

quoted by Eugene Beresin, Christopher Gordon, and
David Herzog, 1989
p. 119

日

Losing Specialness

A prominent theme was a sense at first of losing specialness, only to regain it in other healthier ways:

Self acceptance took its place. I lost my rigid obsessiveness, my robot-type existence. I lost my impatience. I feel safer now. I can believe in my own judgment now and not theirs. People used to take advantage of me. Not anymore. I thought by controlling food, I could control my life concretely, but this was really not the case. Being skinny I felt special. Now it's not being skinny that I feel special. I still feel different from others, but in some positive sense.

I lost nothing. What took its place? Curiosity, laughter, joy, adventure, opening my eyes to what there is and experiencing my feelings.

I didn't have much to lose. What I had to lose was misery and a negative way of thinking and many tears. Nothing was right. I felt driven by anorexia nervosa, slowed down. What took its place? Seeing, hearing, tasting things, mental acuity. This was never present. I can feel now. I miss people now and I enjoy being with them.

I gave up being powerful, I gave up rituals and magic. I gave up laxatives. I gave up my constant stomach problems. I gave up my mother as the perfect mother and being symbiotic with her. Would she survive if we separated? What took its place? I took its place.

> quoted by Eugene Beresin, Christopher Gordon, and
> David Herzog, 1989
> *p. 124*

The Refined Athletic Skill of Vomiting

I WAS THE MISS AMERICA of purging. I was the best. Friends of mine got exhausted after two times. I could do it nine or ten. I could *always* make the food come up. If it wouldn't I would reach down in my throat, open the flap and bring it up! It was amazing what I could do. . . . Some girls felt really good about being a cheerleader. I never felt proud of that like I did about purging. And purging was mine. No one knew about it so they couldn't criticize me for it.

> Susan Sands, 1989
> *p. 80*

A Male Bulimic's Obsession with Food and Suicide

I WAS PHYSICALLY exhausted most of the time, and my hands, feet, and abdomen were frequently puffy and edematous, which I, of course, interpreted as gain in body fat and which contributed to my obsession with weight and food. I weighed myself several times per day in various locations, attending to half pound variations as though my life depended on them. My dreams were often nightmares of dead, rubbery flesh in strips wrapping around me and inserting itself into my mouth. As in graduate school, I alternated thoughts of food with those of suicide, and frequently stared at myself in the mirror while holding a pistol to my head.

quoted by Arnold Andersen, 1990
p. 21

⊒

Teachers Approve of the Anorexic Paragons

AT THIRTEEN, I WAS taking in the caloric equivalent of the food energy available to the famine victims of the siege of Paris. I did my school-work diligently and kept quiet in the classroom. I was a wind-up obedience toy. Not a teacher or principal or guidance counselor confronted me with an objection to my evident deportation in stages from the land of the living.

There were many starving girls in my junior high school, and every one was a teacher's paragon. We were allowed to come and go, racking up gold stars, as our hair fell out in fistfuls and the pads flattened behind the sockets of our eyes. When our eyeballs moved, we felt the resistance. They allowed us to haul our bones around the swinging rope in gym class, where nothing but the force of an exhausted will stood between the ceiling, to which we clung with hands so wasted the jute seemed to abrade the cartilage itself, and the polished wooden floor thirty-five feet below.

An alien voice took mine over. I have never been so soft-spoken. It lost expression and timbre and sank to a monotone, a dull murmur the opposite of strident. My teachers approved of me. They saw nothing wrong with what I was doing, and I could swear they looked straight at me. My school had stopped dissecting alleycats, since it was considered inhumane. There was no interference in my self-directed science experiment: to find out just how little food could keep a human body alive.

Naomi Wolf, 1991
p. 202

17

Psychopharmacology

The Tendency to Leap on the Depressive Bandwagon
Should Be Contained

THE IDEA THAT anorexia nervosa is a variant of depression is gaining increased currency . . . Because we can treat depression successfully, physicians are comfortable with the diagnosis, and a penchant for spreading its net widely is understandable. We propose, however, that the tendency to leap on the depressive bandwagon should be contained in view of the existing uncertainties. Expanding its boundaries may obscure, not clarify, the path to a clear understanding of anorexia nervosa.

Kenneth Altshuler and Myron Weiner, 1985
p. 331

The Healthier Patient Who Can Be Medicated Is Also
More Suitable for Psychotherapy

ONLY THOSE BULIMICS who are well motivated and less regressed can be medicated without the risk of alternate symptom development or acting out; however, it is just such healthier patients who have the most favorable psychotherapeutic prognosis. . . . It must be kept in mind that at best medication may make the patient more amenable to dynamic therapy, but it cannot change the underlying impulsive, masochistic personality disorder.

C. Philip Wilson, 1988
p. 516

己

No Evidence Whatsoever that Medications Alter the Long-Term Outcome of Anorexia Nervosa

AT BEST, MEDICATIONS have a limited role in the current treatment of anorexia nervosa. Although many anecdotal reports have demonstrated the success of one treatment or another, there is no consistent body of evidence suggesting that any one particular type of medication is helpful. Furthermore, the studies that do exist have focused on short-term treatment during which time the goal is, above all, weight gain. There is no evidence whatsoever that medications alter the long-term outcome of anorexia nervosa.

Michael Gitlin, 1990
p. 141

己

Bulimia and Depression Are Not a Single Disorder

THE HYPOTHESIS – THAT bulimia and depression are equivalent – is shaky. Sources of dysphoria in bulimic patients are multiple: depression is mixed with dysphoric mood stemming from poor self-esteem and shame due to the bulimia along with other characterological sources of depressed mood. The marked shifts in weight seen in normal-weight bulimia may also cause some of the biological characteristics of starvation, thereby causing depressive symptoms analogous to those seen in anorexia nervosa. Furthermore, the presence of depression in bulimic patients does not predict a better response to antidepressants in controlling binge frequency. Depression and bulimia, when they coexist, do not necessarily remit together; at times the bingeing may respond to treatment while the depression continues, while at other times the reverse sequence is seen. Overall, then, conceptualizing bulimia and depression as a single disorder with multiple manifestations seems inaccurate. What is more likely is that the two disorders are commonly occurring comorbid conditions, that is, that the presence of one condition (bulimia) makes the presence of the other (depression) more likely, analogous to the frequent co-occurrence of depression and borderline personality disorder.

Michael Gitlin, 1990
p. 144

Collaboration of a Nonphysician Therapist with the Psychopharmacologist

W E USUALLY ATTEMPT to avoid the use of psychotropic medications with this population; however, some patients may display significant Axis I (*DSM-III-R*) symptoms that may be more effectively managed with a brief trial of medication. To reduce splitting when referring and to increase the likelihood of consistency and continuity of care, we recommend the following procedures for the nonphysician therapist. First, the therapist should discuss with the psychiatrist the patient's symptoms and the reasons why the therapist believes medications would be a helpful intervention. Second, if both professionals agree that medication should be considered, they should develop a plan that includes (a) a clear method of communication with the patient about the therapist's concerns; (b) an established appointment date with the psychiatrist; (c) clarification of the role of the psychiatrist with the patient (i.e., the psychiatrist will not take crisis calls, see the patient for ongoing therapy, be viewed as the primary treatment provider, etc.); (d) exploration with the patient about the meaning of and fantasies surrounding a medication trial; and (e) the sanctioning by the patient of ongoing communication between the two professionals.

Amy Baker Dennis and Randy Sansone, 1991
p. 138

己

Beware of Life-Threatening Side Effects

For the general psychiatrist, one therapeutic caveat stands out: Beware of the potential for life-threatening side effects in this patient population. For example, lithium carbonate is potentially toxic to patients who severely restrict food intake or who induce vomiting or abuse laxatives and diuretics. Appreciation of the severe character pathology that may accompany eating disorders should make clinicians cautious in prescribing any drugs that may be taken unreliably, abused, or employed in suicide attempts. In this often fragilely organized patient population, there is no substitute for a good therapeutic alliance and conservative practice.

Kathryn Zerbe, 1992
p. 174

18

Psychotherapy and Psychoanalysis

Reduce the Severity of the Superego

THE AIM THEN, in therapy of this type of case, is to reduce the severity of the superego so that the patient has more feeling of inner freedom, and more flexibility in the outer world, with more capacity to enjoy it. The externalization of aggressive and tender feelings in the analytical situation becomes an important factor because the patient gets for the first time the opportunity to dare to think, talk, and act freely, without being punished, so that feelings of guilt slowly diminish. Thus the ego becomes strengthened as the patient learns to accept impulses previously considered forbidden and guiltful.

Sandor Lorand, 1943
p. 291

Their Fasting, They Must Be Told, Is Merely a Symptom

IT IS ESSENTIAL to tell them, if necessary in the most elementary manner, that their real problem is not food, as everyone else seems to think it is. Their fasting, they must be told, is merely a symptom of their problem, much as a high temperature is a symptom of typhoid. It is only the visible manifestation of something hidden deep in their history, their family problems, their outlook on life, their loneliness, sadness and secret fears. All the therapist can and must do is to aim, not at extracting a spate of psychologically interesting material, not at tangible results or at an outright "cure," but at an honest and respectful understanding of his patients, for only in this way can he hope to offset the negative experiences that lie at the very heart of their so-called remoteness.

Mara Selvini Palazzoli, 1963
p. 112

The Patient Lures the Therapist into Assuming Certain Roles

THE VERY EMOTIONS which the anorectic patient is incapable of accepting or acknowledging in herself may appear in her physician's attitude toward her. Instead of becoming aware of positive and negative feelings toward her physician, she tries to lure him into assuming certain roles. The more successful she is in inducing him to pamper or punish her, the more chaotic the situation becomes, since the physician, in "counteraction," exhibits the very same emotional impulses which the patient has to fend off within herself.

Helmut Thomä, 1967
p. 447

Highly Individualistic Personalities Emerge

THERE IS NOTHING more rewarding than seeing these narrow, rigid, isolated creatures change into warm, spontaneous human beings with a wide range of interests and an active participation in life. During the illness they looked and behaved as if they were constructed from the same erector set, mouthing the same stereotyped phrases from the same broken record. It is truly exciting to see the emergence of highly individualistic personalities after these years of sterile self-absorption.

Hilde Bruch, 1978
p. 158

己

The Therapeutic Task Is to Increase Capacity to Cope

T HE THERAPEUTIC task is (1) to enlarge her experience of herself as she is, and usually for her family to attempt the same; (2) to provide her, and often them, with new experiences facilitating personal growth—a growing capacity to cope with herself in life, biologically mature and without recourse to anorexia nervosa.

Arthur H. Crisp, 1980
p. 99

己

No Unitary Treatment

T HERE IS NO unitary treatment for anorexia nervosa. The therapeutic approach to the anorectic depends on a genetic-structural assessment, the level of her fixation and regression, the primitiveness of her defenses, the extent of the family's pathology, and her ego assets which auger well for a therapeutic response.

John Sours, 1980
p. 370

己

How Anorexics Differ from Other Patients in Therapy

W HEN THEY ARRIVE, they are unable to form a therapeutic alliance or to test realistically their personal relationships. The initial part of the treatment must work toward the overcoming of these difficulties. These patients differ from the average psychiatric patient in the following:

1. They have no experience (like most schizoid personalities) with human relationships. At best they have had friendly acquaintances and kind superiors. The therapist is the first person with whom they begin to talk about themselves.
2. They arrive as nonverbal people and have a limited ability to use language, describe events, themselves, or others, even when they can be very sophisticated in intellectual matters.
3. They are unable to obtain any pleasure in their relationships with others.
4. They do not know how to play and have a very limited capacity to symbolize and fantasize.
5. They do not believe that any human being can take any interest in them beyond their appearance or performance. This is a specific impediment to the formation of a therapeutic alliance.
6. They and their families are very poor historians. It is impossible to obtain from them more than global descriptions of events. Their life appears as a colorless continuation of routine events. From the patients one hears of their performing for others, attempting to be perfect, longing to be recognized and seen, and feeling totally impotent to influence others; from the parents one senses that they have not noticed anything unusual in the child but see only happiness, good behavior, average development, and, after decompensation, incomprehensible stubbornness.
7. The patients' conscious mental life is devoted to the obsessive surveillance of their performance, ruminations about food, their bodies, weight, and how they are seen by others. Their conscious fantasy life is nil. These patients do not daydream. Particularly conspicuous is the restriction of their sense of time to the present. Their past is summed up in a few sentences. They do not examine their life, they have it.

Ana-Maria Rizzuto, Ross K. Peterson, and Marilyn Reed, 1981
p. 478

An Anorexic Needs Help in Her Search for Autonomy and Self-Directed Identity

THE QUESTION "whom treatment is for" needs to be clarified from the onset, that it is for the benefit and development of the patient, not something to appease the parents. An anorexic needs help in her search for autonomy and self-directed identity. An important aspect of the therapeutic relationship is that what she has to say is listened to and made the object of exploration. A common problem in her background is that things, usually of a positive nature, were done according to the parents' decision without regard for the child's expressed wishes and needs. Focus needs to be on her failure in self experience, on the defective tools and concepts for organizing and expressing needs. Therapy aims at liberating patients from the distorting influence of early experiences and from the errors of their convictions so that they can discover that they have substance and worth and do not need the strained and stressful superstructure of artificial perfection.

Hilde Bruch, 1982a
p. 6

At the Beginning of Therapy, Explain that the Eating Disorder Is a Cover-up for Underlying Problems

AT THE BEGINNING of treatment it is useful to give a simple dynamic explanation of the meaning of the illness—that the preoccupation with eating and weight is a cover-up for underlying problems and patients' doubt about their own worth and value, that they need help to discover their good qualities and assets, and that at this stage the severe starvation interferes with their psychological processes. It is important to clarify from the outset that the goal of psychotherapy is to accomplish something for the patient's benefit and not to appease the parents.

Hilde Bruch, 1982b
p. 1536

己

Anorexic Patients Need Help in Giving Up Their Dichotomous Thinking

PSYCHOTHERAPY MUST gradually help the patient develop realistic expectations and a sense that there are alternatives to the polarization of experiences in different areas of her life. She must learn to question her own assumption that if she moves a small distance on a continuum of change, she has assumed the opposite position to that held earlier. The patient must slowly begin to recognize when she is using this style of thinking with its maladaptive consequences, and how to question its validity by examining contradictory evidence from her own experiences. One 22-year-old patient provided an illustration of dichotomous reasoning in the evaluation of her parents. Initially she praised them unconditionally for their loving devotion to their children. During one visit to her parents' home, the patient was overwhelmed by panic and guilt at the realization that her mother was not completely altruistic and wise. This patient painfully recognized only then that her mother did not accept shortcomings in any of her children but preferred to deny the presence of any faults. She discovered that her panic related to her evaluation of her mother in totally "good" or "bad" terms (splitting). Any awareness of fault meant complete rejection and a fear of retaliation. She found it difficult to perceive that both she and her mother possessed a mixture of positive and negative qualities. This understanding was not the end of the patient's tendency to view her mother (or herself) in binary terms but it was an experience that could be referred to again during the course of psychotherapy.

Dichotomous reasoning can also be observed in patients' vacillation between overcompliance and stubbornness with an inability to assume a more moderate position. Accomplishments are approached in extreme terms. A major therapeutic task lies in helping the patient to understand that it is self-defeating to approach every aspect of life in "all-or-nothing" terms.

P. E. Garfinkel, D. M. Garner and K. Bemis, 1982
p. 272

⊇

The Patient Is Constantly Pulling Back

T HE PATIENT constantly is pulling back towards the silent kind of deadly paralysis and near complete passivity. When these lively parts of the patient remain so constantly split off it means that his whole capacity for wanting and appreciating, missing, feeling disturbed at losing, etc., the very stuff that makes for real whole object relating is projected and the patient remains with his addiction and without the psychological means of combatting this.

Betty Joseph, 1982
p. 454

⊇

All the Active Parts of the Patient Are Projected

T HE ANALYST seems to be the only person in the room who is actively concerned about change, about progress, about development, as if all the active parts of the patient have been projected into the analyst.

Betty Joseph, 1982
p. 454

⊇

Acting Out Is Part of Treatment

V ERY FREQUENTLY, derivatives of a conflict seem to have to be acted out in outside life and in the transference before the conflict and its accompanying fantasies can be brought into treatment.

Charles C. Hogan, 1983c
p. 212

Abandoning the Anorexia Results in Considerable Anxiety

T HESE PATIENTS do not wish to deal with or discuss the true problems that exist in their lives, but rather, to speak continually about eating, dieting, and weight loss. Once they begin to recognize and accept that the preoccupation with eating and dieting in part is used to avoid dealing with real-life problems, the anorexia may begin to abate. Indeed, once these patients decide to abandon the anorexia, they frequently feel considerable anxiety about how to deal with the problems their anorexic preoccupations had masked.

Ira Mintz, 1983c
p. 89

Starving Binds the Patients' Conflicts

A NOREXIC PATIENTS frequently report that they have nothing to talk about and that there is nothing that troubles them. This results from their conscious withholding of all vital thoughts and feelings because they do not trust the therapist. In addition, not eating tends to bind the patients' conflicts defensively. Once patients begin to eat, they often report feeling flooded by all kinds of upsetting ideas—which can be so frightening that the patient returns to her starvation. After beginning to eat, one patient reported being so upset by the emerging ideas that he could not sleep. Another commented that she was afraid of going crazy.

Ira Mintz, 1983c
p. 90

⊒

The Therapist's Sole Interest Is to Understand Their Problems rather than Make Them Eat

IN THE EARLY phase of treatment, it is very important that the therapist be dissociated from authority figures and convince patients that his or her sole interest is to understand their problems, rather than to make them eat or to control them. Patients who are in danger of dying require hospitalization and treatment by the pediatrician or internist to help them recover from the emergency, but once they are out of medical danger, treatment should focus primarily on problems and conflicts, not eating.

Ira Mintz, 1983c
p. 98

⊒

Be Active

TECHNICALLY, IT IS advisable to be more active, talkative, and open with teenage patients than with adult patients. With anorexia patients specifically, it is often helpful to interpret resistances and conflict earlier, especially when patients are on a rapid downhill course.

Ira Mintz, 1983c
p. 111

⊒

It Is an Error to Wait

IT IS AN ERROR to wait with these patients for the transference and alliance slowly to develop, just as it is ill-advised to wait for the emergence of clear, obvious material prior to interpreting it. Anorexic patients may die before they talk because they are so self-destructive, so unused to revealing thoughts and feelings by speaking, and so prone to act out conflicts through symptoms.

Ira Mintz, 1983d
p. 220

Patients' Punitive Superego Determines the Sequence of Dealing with Conflicts

In DEALING WITH the conflicts of anorexic patients, it is better to deal with those over aggression prior to those surrounding sexuality and to deal with the self-destructive aspects of the aggression before the destructive aspects. This sequence seems most amenable to these patients' strict, primitive, punitive superego, with its tendency for immediate self-punishment via symptom formation for imagined transgressions.

Ira Mintz, 1983d
p. 227

Quiet Tolerance of Uncertainty

In THE END it is the analyst's own quiet tolerance of the muddle and uncertainty, of the gradualness of approximation, of error and apology that make it possible for his patient to come simply to be. In being resides the experience that when genuinely experienced leads to the insights with which development is facilitated. The capacity for both parties to the analysis to manage the presence of the absence of certainty is what, more I think than anything, to be or not be the conducive factor.

Harold Boris, 1984a
p. 435

Respond Empathically as Subject, Not as Target

In all the initial stages of therapy, one cannot overestimate the importance of establishing empathic contact by responding as subject rather than target of the patient's feelings, for such interaction allows the patient to feel understood. To respond as the subject of the patient's needs means that when she laments about the unfairness of the staff or her parents, we apprehend and explore how it feels to be so misunderstood, not how distorted are her perceptions; when she feels enraged at us, we explore with her those specifics of our behavior which made her feel so furious, not interpret the transference distortions of her anger; when she describes her power struggles with family and staff, we explore how it feels to experience the world as a constant battle for control, not delineate her provocative behavior.

Richard Geist, 1985
p. 279

Empathic Response to Compliance as a Resistance

Nowhere is the destructive use of behavioral principles more apparent than in the unwitting reinforcement of compliant behavior. For compliance in the anorexic patient — as in most narcissistic patients — represents an abortive attempt to substitute environmental directives, therapeutic interpretations, or parental wishes for the missing structure of the self. Such compliance, rather than being reinforced through any kind of token economy or intrusive interpretation, must be responded to in the same empathic manner described above. First, we must acknowledge the patient's attempts to comply with our wishes. Second, we must recognize with the patient that such compliance helps her to feel whole and alive because it provides self-definition. Third, we must explore with the patient her lifelong pattern of self-defining submission. Fourth, we must recognize the painful conflict inherent in compliance — how the patient wants to please in order to gain self-definition, while simultaneously resenting her compliance. And fifth, we must help the patient to understand the motivation for compliance—her intense fear of fragmentation and empty depletion when she fails to experience herself as whole. In my experience, such an empathic response to compliance as a resistance leads automatically to the patient's interest in rekindling the lost elements of the self.

Richard Geist, 1985
p. 280

Address the Broken Narcissistic Bond

W HEN EMPATHIC connectedness between patient and therapist is broken, many therapists seem to panic and institute unwarranted and austere limit-setting interventions through intrusive interpretation, behavioral manipulation, active physical restraint, and forced feeding. While hospitalization, IV hyperalimentation, and restriction may at times be medically necessary, the active psychotherapeutic stance should be interpretation addressed to the interpersonal events which had temporarily broken the narcissistic bond between patient and therapist.

Richard Geist, 1985
p. 285

Clarify the Developmental Deficits

W E MUST CONTINUE to patiently clarify the developmental deficits which contribute to the syndrome of anorexia. Only through such continuing clarification can we delineate the quality of the therapeutic relationship and specific treatment techniques which help to rekindle the lost elements of the self, without precipitately substituting weight for emerging selfhood.

Richard A. Geist, 1985
p. 287

⊐

Similarity in the Symptoms Hides the Range of Level of Object Relations at which These Patients Are Functioning

CLINICAL EXPERIENCE suggests that there is a range of level of object relations functioning in these patients that may be obscured by the superficial similarity in the symptoms they present. . . . Engaging these patients in therapy, establishing and maintaining a treatment alliance, and making effective psychotherapeutic interventions present different technical problems depending on the level of object relations at which the patient is functioning.

Joyce Kraus Aronson, 1986
p. 669

⊐

Facilitating Effects of the Holding Environment

CONTINUOUSLY STRUGGLING to maintain a sense (often illusionary) of autonomy and self-sufficiency, to communicate feelings raises the danger of humiliation and annihilation of their fragile sense of self. Because of these considerations, what is called for during the initial phase of treatment is an empathic acceptance and awareness of the patient's pain, interpretations that are perceived as empathic, and quietly waiting. Although during this period the therapist might sense that little is happening, the treatment process has already been set in motion by the facilitating effects of the holding environment.

Howard Lerner, 1986
p. 42

⊇

Appreciate the Adaptive Necessity of the Patient's Denial

PUSHING A PATIENT too quickly to give up her self-denying stance will invariably be met with considerable resistance. This fact was driven home to me most poignantly when I first started working with eating disordered patients and was conducting a large number of intake evaluations. After a while I became quite "skilled" at discovering and pointing out to patients the traumatic patterns in the family relationships that may have contributed to the inexplicable development of their eating symptoms. Such interpretive efforts often did result in dramatic "breakthroughs" during the interview in which the patient was suddenly overwhelmed by her feelings—usually relating to some intolerable aspect of her family situation. What was surprising and disturbing was that many of the patients never followed up in treatment after these intense intake sessions. In retrospect, my understanding of this is that I failed to adequately appreciate the adaptive necessity of these patients' denial and self-denial. For them to be confronted with, and consciously experience, their denied needs and feelings with respect to their families was itself a form of *unacceptable individuation* that was too threatening to them without an established treatment alliance.

Steven Stern, 1986
p. 246

⊇

Changing the Patient's Experience of the Therapist's Empathic Failure

EACH TIME WE explored something she experienced as an empathic failure on my part, Patricia became more comfortable recognizing her own needs and feelings and modulating them by talking about them and asking for what she needed from me rather than by bingeing on food and/or sex and then feeling worse than before about herself. As she found herself able to discuss her needs with me, and to find ways of getting those needs met (sometimes simply *discussing* her needs met them), her self-esteem increased, her ability to tolerate not always getting her needs met increased, and her bingeing and purging decreased gradually.

Diane Barth, 1988
p. 277

ⅎ

Multiple Meanings of Symptoms

Not only can the same symptom have different meanings for different individuals, but the same symptom can also have different meanings for the same individual at different times. It is therefore important for a therapist to try to understand the meaning a symptom has for a specific individual at a specific moment without imposing an "experience-distant" theoretical stance on the client's experience.

Diane Barth, 1988
p. 272

ⅎ

Anorexics Do Not Complain about Their Condition, They Glory in It

On principle, anorexic patients resist treatment and remain uncommitted to therapy for a long time. They do not complain about their condition; on the contrary, they glory in it. They are reluctant to let go of the "security" of their cadaverous existence. They feel they have found, in their extreme thinness, the perfect solution to all their problems, that it makes them feel better and helps them to attain the respect and admiration they have yearned for all their lives. Only reluctantly do they deal with the underlying erroneous assumptions that are the preconditions for this self-deceptive pseudosolution.

Hilde Bruch, 1988
p. 7

己

Every Anorexic Feels Fundamentally Inadequate

THROUGH WORK with many patients, I have been impressed that an anorexic's whole life is based on certain misconceptions that need to be exposed and corrected in therapy. Deep down, every anorexic is convinced that basically she is inadequate, low, mediocre, inferior, and despised by others. She lives in an imaginary world with an assumed reality where she feels that people around her—her family, her friends, and the world at large—look down on her with disapproving eyes, ready to pounce on her with criticism. The image of human behavior and interaction that an anorexic constructs in her apparently well-functioning home is one of surprising cynicism, pessimism, and bitterness. All her efforts, her striving for perfection and excessive thinness, are directed toward hiding the fatal flaw of her fundamental inadequacy.

Hilde Bruch, 1988
p. 6

己

Therapist's Coercion Replicates Parental Coercion

FOR THE SYMPTOMS of eating disorders to be effectively alleviated, interpretation must be combined, when and where appropriate, with active assistance from the therapist in forming and carrying out individually tailored, specific, achievable goals that will begin to replace the patient's desperate inner struggle for control with a growing sense of mastery. On the other hand, task-oriented treatment without clarification, empathic mirroring, interpretation, transference analysis, and all the other aspects of sensitive psychoanalytic treatment will again leave the patient feeling that she or he is being coerced into meeting the needs of a demanding parent rather than being appropriately understood and nurtured.

Harriet Goldman, 1988
p. 565

⊐

Structural Changes Are Needed, Not Simply Symptomatic Relief

IF THE GOAL IS that of bringing about significant structural change, rather than pure symptomatic relief, psychoanalytic exploration is not only indicated but necessary.

Remi Gonzalez, 1988
p. 438

⊐

A More Active Interpretive Stance with the Starving Anorexic and the Markedly Self-Destructive Bulimic

DURING THE FIRST ten sessions, endless self-punishing thoughts and behavior were described as an integral part of her past and current life experience. It was repeatedly pointed out that unconsciously getting herself in trouble was a desperate attempt to get people to care for and pay attention to her. On occasion it was also an expression of anger in an attempt to upset and aggravate them through hurting herself. She was punishing herself because her strict, rigid conscience required that she suffer; she did not deserve to have a good opinion of herself nor to achieve happiness and success in life. Pointing out the ego adaptive function of the thoughts and behavior, as well as punitive superego aspects, are well tolerated by patients from the very beginning of treatment, where a more active interpretive stance is required especially in the starving anorexic or in the markedly self-destructive bulimic.

Ira Mintz, 1988
p. 147

⊐

It Is Inadvisable to Encourage the Patient to Renounce the Eating Behavior

THE AWARENESS that starving or gorging both tend to displace conflict to the preoccupation with food and the subsiding of the original problem, provides the therapist with the opportunity to emphasize the secondary gain provided by the symptom. Thus, one is not forced into the inadvisable position of attempting to encourage the patient to renounce the eating behavior, which only tends to set off defiance or the sense of being controlled. Instead, it is possible to point out that if the patient is willing to face and to deal effectively with the problems, the need to avoid them by starving or gorging will subside.

Ira Mintz, 1988
p. 155

The Patient Sets the Pace

SOME PATIENTS will not tolerate the least criticism of their parents, even when they themselves have become increasingly aware of the negative aspects of their home life. In such cases it is always best to sit back while the patient solves the problem at her own pace.

Mara Selvini Palazzoli, 1988
p. 176

Words that Are Premature Will Be Vomited

THE ANALYST must remember that words do not mean anything and that more than in any other analytic situation, careful and respectful naming of feelings, empathic understanding of the patient's need to reject the analyst's interventions, and interpretation of defense must precede interpretation of content. Words that are premature will be vomited. The analyst must remember that the patient is trying to avoid the repetition of trauma and that the analytic tool, the analyst's words, may activate in the patient the defenses that are to be overcome. The narrow margin that the pathology leaves for the analyst, and the very strong defenses against affective contact, make the bulimarexics the most difficult and refractory anorexic patients.

Ana-Maria Rizzuto, 1988
p. 385

☲

Drives, Defenses, and Object Relations from All Developmental Levels Need Analytic Attention

THE INTERPRETIVE point of urgency varies from session to session and moment to moment. Drives, defenses, and object relations from all developmental levels need analytic attention as they approach affective-preconscious accessibility. For some, dependency on mother does represent a (bilateral) failure of separation. For most, however, an exclusive focus on the conflicts from below obfuscates the defensive elements in the negative oedipal constellation. Clinging to mother always includes the defensive function of retreating from competing with her.

Harvey Schwartz, 1988
p. 48

☲

The Early Treatment Relationship Can Be Chaotic

EFFORTS AT PSYCHOANALYTIC therapy are often aborted because of the intense and seemingly chaotic dyadic relationship that characterizes the early work with these difficult patients.

Newell Fischer, 1989
p. 42

Focus on the Symptom Limits Our Capacity to Listen

ONE APPROACH IS to define the symptom as the disease. It is the enemy, so we must launch a battle. The symptom must be destroyed. This approach is flawed in several respects. It neglects the function of the symptom in maintaining psychological equilibrium. It also confirms the anal perspective of the bulimic's world: there is a badness within that must be purged. Therapy then becomes another repetition of the purging process, with its inevitable price of humiliation. Like the symptom, a purgative therapy may be partially successful to contain the patient's world, but does little to heal a fragmented self. In fact it confirms this fragmentation. Such approaches could be seen as our own theoretical symptom-formations, restrictive attempts to organize our explorations that limit our capacity to listen openly to the patient.

Paul Hamburg, 1989
p. 137

Many Fragile and Borderline Patients Are Capable of Engaging in an Exciting, Creative and Rewarding Psychoanalytic Experience

ON THE BASIS of symptoms alone we have little insight into the direction an individual's analytic voyage will take. Many a so-called "good neurotic" may prove intractably unanalyzable while many a narcissistically fragile, borderline, or polysomatizing patient is capable of engaging in an exciting, creative and rewarding psychoanalytic experience.

Joyce McDougall, 1989
p. 8

The Analysis of Relapses May Reveal Early
Traumatic Experience

EXPERIENCES OF severing oneself from an addiction are rich in discovery in the course of the analytic voyage. Since relapses are the rule rather than the exception, the analysand may be interested in exploring the narcissistic and libidinal wounds that precipitate an addictive plunge. The analysis of such experiences may reveal the early traumatic experiences of infancy and the personality organization and psychic economy which subsequently developed, leaving the child (and the future adult) without adequate inner resources for coping with emotional flooding.

Joyce McDougall, 1989
p. 98

When the Mind Is Able to Take Over, the Body Becomes
Relieved of Its Attempts to Find a Solution

EACH PATIENT, using the soma's complex translation of the psyche's messages, reveals a different drama. When its theme can be told, and shared, in the therapeutic situation—for the work of analysis is always a story recreated by two people—the mind is able to take over the task of modifying the drama. In so doing, the body becomes relieved of its repetitive attempts to find a solution to psychic pain.

Joyce McDougall, 1989
p. 171

Interpreting Compliance

The Patient: I felt the need, while away, to force myself to have a powerful insight that would push me beyond this anorectic morass, this morbid fear of eating, so that I can grow physically and emotionally and give up clinging to this little girl way of life. I had such an insight and, as I was arriving at your house, I had the phantasy that I tell you this wonderful insight and you pull out a gun and shoot me in the head. It's so real I am still shaking. We were visiting my parents and my niece was there as usual. As I watched Luke be with Willa with great skill, warmth, and love, bringing out the best in her, I thought, "Her gain is not his loss and they each clearly know this." This is the opposite of how it was with my parents and me. As I heard my father, who loves Willa very much, refer to her as "my little girl," I cringed remembering that that was just what he used to say to me and I felt compelled to stay his little girl to retain his love, and still do.

That night I had a dream. Father and I are sitting at the kitchen table, he in pajamas and I in a nightgown, sneaking a snack together while Mother is up in the bedroom. My father was drinking whiskey (which he never does) and getting drunk. He started to pour another glass and I put my hand on his to try to stop him. He then picked me up to take me to the bathroom, saying he had to pee. I was becoming alarmed. He then exposed his erect penis and rubbed it against me. I screamed and ran to get Mother. She angrily accused me of seducing him. I pleaded with her and her response was, "I know he isn't that sexually capable by himself." I felt my heart sink; there was nowhere to turn. This is horrible, really horrible. I was startled by the directness of the dream. No disguises. I can't grow up. I have to stay Father's little girl to retain his love. If Mother sees my maturing femininity as a threat to her own, she is filled with jealousy and attacks me as a dangerous rival, so I have to retreat. Well, this is my insight (spoken with trembling voice). I guess it's not so great after all.

I ask why she undoes her accomplishment. Why so fearful of my response? "You will be like my mother. Insights are yours. If I claim them, you will be jealous and shoot me," she answers.

"You have to stay a little girl for Father's favor, unwomanly for Mother's, and anorectic to be my interesting and compliant patient," I comment.

Excitedly, she says, "Yes, yes. Last year, without realizing it, I was forcing you to continue to be available to me even on vacation by being so worrisomely anorectic. Thank God, I am beyond that now."

S. Louis Mogul, 1989
p. 82

己

Reintegrating Psyche and Soma

W HAT IS REQUIRED in this work is that the analyst hold and handle both the anorexic's psyche and soma in a manner that will allow him to constantly introduce and reintroduce these dissociated aspects of her experience to one another, and thereby facilitate their reintegration. This process does not, of course, involve actually physically holding and handling of the patient by the analyst. It is achieved instead through the holding and handling inherent in the provision of tactful interpretations that follow empathic understanding of the anorexic's experience of her psyche and soma.

James Sacksteder, 1989a
p. 410

己

Anorexics Are Quick to Feel Unrealistically Discouraged and Often Produce This Same Feeling in Their Therapist

A NOREXICS, ESPECIALLY when they are first beginning to change, are prone to feel that lapses into old behaviors imply that they have not changed at all, in any way, and they feel terrible about this. It is a dedifferentiated view of change that parallels the anorexic's inclination toward dedifferentiated affects and toward inhuman standards of achievement. They are very let down by themselves, and they quickly become unrealistically discouraged, frustrated, and depressed, and feel hopeless and helpless about ever effecting any lasting change in themselves. In addition, they are also quite good at convincing others, including their therapist and the nurses involved with their treatment, that all is lost; they engender the same feelings of total defeat and discouragement in others that they themselves feel. This can lead all parties concerned to seriously consider ending the treatment because of the mistaken impression of a lack of progress.

James Sacksteder, 1989a
p. 419

The Therapist Must Withhold "Brilliant" Perceptions

THE INFANTILE ROLE which the patient predictably assigns to the therapist, that of omniscient, non-adaptive, and monologic maternal replica, is readily sensed and must be repeatedly, firmly and openly acknowledged but then declined, permitting the disclosure of her central ignorance of her perceptual life. In turn, this facilitates the emergence of a more regressed and turbulent range of phenomena, much less brittle and smoothed over than the more familiar parroted presentation. The therapist must "become able to wait and wait for the natural evolution of the transference" according to Winnicott (1971), and to withhold "brilliant" or "original" perceptions, which rarely contribute. The patient may then be able to sense the therapist's awareness of and respect for her adaptive and economic need of her illness and to embark on identifying and piecing together self-observations on her own, that is to say, as original with her rather than as not-me intrusions to be repulsed.

R. Ian Story, 1990
p. 6

The Role of the Family Physician

THE FAMILY PHYSICIAN usually makes the diagnosis of . . . [anorexia nervosa] and can play an important supportive role in therapy. It is important that he emphasize to the parents and the anorexic patient the serious, possibly fatal, nature of this disease while advising psychodynamic treatment for the members of the anorexic family unit. In the course of therapy, the family physician can fulfill an invaluable role in backing up treatment, quieting the parents' fears about their child's health by appropriate examinations, and deciding in consultation with the [therapist] when hospitalization is necessary if the anorexic patient induces a starvation crisis.

The family physician should understand that the [anorexic patient] is in intense conflict about eating and that unless the patient's weight is at a dangerous level, it is best to prescribe a reasonable diet but to leave the issue of eating or not eating for the patient to bring up in her psychotherapy. Attempts to coerce or force the patient to eat can result in a sadistic refusal to eat.

C. Philip Wilson, 1990
p. 248

Patients Fear that Psychotherapy Will Disrupt Their Sense of Themselves

No MATTER HOW much an individual may hope that therapy will help her, she will also fear (either consciously or unconsciously) that it will disrupt the very sense of herself that her symptoms help her maintain.

Diane Barth, 1991
p. 226

Identification with the Therapist's Empathic Stance

The THERAPIST'S empathy is often a novel experience for many individuals with eating disorders, who have never before felt that someone else was actively attempting to understand their perspective. They are often highly critical of their own feelings and thoughts and therefore unable to empathize with themselves. The capacity to empathize with themselves is also hindered by an inability to formulate their own thoughts and feelings. Thus an important part of the therapeutic work involves an identification with the therapist's stance, and the subsequent development of empathy for their own feelings and needs. Such "self" empathy is necessary for the feelings to be articulated, recognized, and integrated into an individual's overall sense of self.

Diane Barth, 1991
p. 226

己

The Patient Offers No Materials with which to Build
Either Boat or Shelter

ONCE I ASKED HER, in what appeared to be a more relaxed moment, about her fantasies of suicide through starvation; had they subsided? "Oh no," she responded, "if they had, I wouldn't have minded talking about them." She told me during another meeting: "If something were important, of course I wouldn't say it." Clearly, Lisa had carved out a province on which we could meet, an island as remote and as confining as the one on which we encounter so many of our anorexic clients, an island desolate enough to afford no materials with which to build either boat or shelter and, most important, one on which she herself was the force that held us both captive. As I was piecing together an understanding of her experience, she was already preparing to banish me, as a ruler exiles those with access to state secrets in order to consolidate control. And so a pattern evolved: the more there was to talk about, the less there was to say. Lisa's daily life was filled with the sort of overwhelming obstacles that might be expected to confront any individual who had been raised with all of the ambition and imperatives for success, but none of the support or guidance that would allow her to fulfill them. She made an imaginary list each Friday morning as she walked to her session of the things she needed to talk about—the realistically quite frightening fears, symptoms, and fantasies that she had come to live with as a result of her predicament. Rarely did I hear of these. Instead, she appeared to emerge from each meeting with a feeling of victory, knowing that she had once again prevailed against her temptation to say that which she most desperately needed to say, again secure in her sense of herself as lost and yet strong, empowered and quite alone.

Nancy Burke, 1991
p. 153

The Therapist Must Be Committed, Consistent, Durable, and Reliable

THE TYPE OF healing therapeutic relationship that is necessary with these [borderline bulimic] patients takes years, perhaps decades, rather than months to develop. Consequently, the therapist needs to be careful with both his or her and the patients' ambitiousness regarding symptom remission in order to protect against the harsh, critical, often masochistic fallout that can occur from the patients' feelings of failure.

The pathway to developing a healing therapeutic relationship with borderline bulimics is simultaneously simple and quite complicated. The primary task, from my perspective, is to demonstrate to the patients over the course of time that the therapist is committed, consistent, durable, and reliable.

Craig Johnson, 1991
p. 182

Understanding Conflicts in Terms of Ego Strivings for Separation-Individuation Often Facilitates Maturation

FOCUS ON SEXUAL and aggressive fantasies as ends in themselves can often lead to interminable analysis and failure of resolution. Understanding and translation of such conflicts into terms of ego strivings, developmental efforts toward resolution of the problems involved in separation-individuation, often will make for significant maturational development and relief of anorexic symptoms.

Cecil Mushatt, 1992
p. 302

19

Sociocultural Issues

The Cultural Ideal Has Shifted toward a
Thinner Size

THERE HAS BEEN A gradual but definite evolution in the cultural ideal body shape for women over the past 20 years. Particularly within the past 10 years, there has been a shift in the ideal standard toward a thinner size. The results from both the *Playboy* centerfolds and the Miss America Pageant contestants confirm and quantify this trend. The *Playboy* data further indicate that bust, waist, and hip measurements have evolved toward a more "tubular" body form, although this may be a controversial matter among avid readers. It could be argued that the *Playboy* data simply reflect the changing tastes of the magazine editor, however, the convergent Miss America results suggest a genuine trend. It is also noteworthy that in the past decade the Pageant winners have almost invariably been thinner than the average contestant. Moreover, a simple visual comparison with the models portrayed in "high" fashion magazines suggests that the data sources from this study provide a conservative estimate of the current idealized shape for women. The movement toward a thinner shape for the ideal standard of beauty is more notable considering that, due to improved nutrition, the average female under 30 years of age has become heavier in the past 20 years according to the recently revised actuarial statistics.

D. M. Garner, P. E. Garfinkel, D. Schwartz, and
M. Thompson, 1980
p. 489

⊒

Anorexia Nervosa Is a Leitmotif of the Cultural Forces in Our Society

THE HISTORY OF anorexia nervosa is a history of world psychiatry. It clearly shows how psychiatry has advanced from descriptions of signs and symptoms, diagnostic formulations, studies on the interphase between body and mind, to psychoanalytic views of character and human development. Because of the anorectic's tortured and en-meshing family, the disturbance provides opportunities to examine disorders of family communication and structure.

Anorexia nervosa has become a symbol and leitmotif of the cultural forces in our society. The will to master and control one's selfhood and achieve absolute separateness and autonomy has become, for many Americans, the emblem of a safe existence. We find now a character style, exaggerated in the characterological structure of the anorectic, accentuating control and mastery with the central theme of realiza-tion of an ideal self, ideal body.

John Sours, 1980
p. xiv

⊒

Affluent Cultures Make More Social Demands on Children

CHILDREN REARED IN more affluent cultures are apt to be pushed more quickly into adulthood. Middle-class families make more parental and social demands on their children. Developmental issues of separation-individuation and autonomy are more difficult to negotiate in our society, where precocious growth, premature stimulation, repeated early separations, and increasing responsibility go hand in hand. It is clear that there are psychosocial forces in Western culture that favor the syndrome, as in Japan, where Westernization has apparently increased the incidence of anorexia nervosa.

John Sours, 1980
p. 281

⊒

Anorectics Feel Vulnerable to Loss of Control and Intrusion by Outside Forces

PEOPLE ARE NO longer able to deny death and now are preoccupied with its eventuality; societal and cultural institutions are no longer trusted; societal and group ego-ideals do not mitigate a sense of insecurity; relationships are shallow and open to exploitation; narcissistic therapies have replaced religion in celebration of the self; and, believing that they and society have no future, parents ignore the needs of their children and struggle to find themselves in marriages that soon dissolve. These factors and others blur the boundaries of the self, make people feel vulnerable to passivity, loss of control, and liable to intrusion, invasion, and control by vague, outside forces. Anorectics dread obliteration by the outside world—a fear represented by food.

John Sours, 1980
p. 283

⊒

In Our Culture Men Are Permitted an Abundance of Flesh

FOR THE MAN in this culture, abundance of flesh does not invariably signify that there is something wrong with him and that he has become, for those who love and cherish him, a source of shame. Even when he gains a great deal of weight, becomes what we regard as fat and therefore asserts the undeniable fact of fleshly existence, we do not shrink away from him and find him an object worthy of scorn. There is, for instance, the fat man most familiar in this culture as the millionaire, whose vest bulges and whose gold watch pokes out from his straining pocket, a figure of prestige and influence, whose size reflects his power.

Kim Chernin, 1981
p. 122

己

A Desire to Erase the Memory of the Primordial Mother

WHEN WE ATTEMPT to determine the size and shape of a woman's body, instructing it to avoid its largeness and softness and roundness and girth, we are driven by the desire to expunge the memory of the primordial mother who ruled over our childhood with her inscrutable power over life and death. And we are driven by the longing to erase the past when we decide to impose our will upon a woman's body, inventing an ideal slenderness that will spare us a confrontation with whatever reminds us of the helplessness of our infancy. Above all, in an age when woman asserts her right to autonomy and power, we may be driven to evolve a cultural ideal that will release us from the dangers of remembering.

Kim Chernin, 1981
p. 143

己

Our Culture's Vision of Thinness Is an Illness

WHEN WE LOOK at the anorexic girl, admiring her discipline and asceticism; when we gaze with envy at her as she passes us in the theater, proudly swishing her narrow hips, it is the triumph of her will we are admiring. But we are all so caught up in this struggle against the flesh that we believe we behold beauty in this evidence of the body's emaciation. It is by now, in this culture, virtually impossible for us to see beyond the dictates of this standard. Our obsession has taken possession of our vision of the world. A woman can be neither too wealthy nor too slender, we are told. And we agree. But this vision is an illness we share with the anorexic girl.

Kim Chernin, 1981
p. 48

⊒

Both Hysteria and Anorexia Are Heavily Influenced by the Socio-Cultural Context

W E ARE NOT accustomed to think of mental disorders as political issues, or as cultural by-products. Therefore, it is useful to consider the analogy of classical conversion hysteria, about which Freud wrote in his early career. This, too, was a disease found almost exclusively in women. It, too, mimicked certain social roles—particularly the futility and helplessness—that women of that day were supposed to fill. There is a striking parallel between the "belle indifference" of the classical conversion hysteria and the denial of emaciation found in many anorectics. The hysteric was often quite indifferent to the limb paralysis which was the symptom masking some underlying conflict. Freud would consider a symptom such as a hand paralysis to be a conflict masking the urge to masturbate, for example. We now know that Freud was only partially correct. However, we see in the anorectic how the emaciation often denies the intense bulimic urges, and that the symptoms take a socially acceptable form—dietary and weight consciousness. The anorectic, in her relentless pursuit of thinness, attempts both to satisfy society's demands and to deny or temporize powerful internal needs.

We are not suggesting that anorexia is the modern day form of hysteria, but that both may be emotional disorders whose form and content were and are heavily influenced by the socio-cultural context in which they are observed. This does not seem too ambitious a statement. Both involve the formation of symptoms whose function is to signal distress while symbolizing the underlying wish or impulse.

The particular taboo impulse in each case appears to be determined by the norms of the time. The hysteria analogy for anorexia is so apt, precisely because we can see, in retrospect, how the sexually repressive atmosphere of the culture influenced the formation of hysterical symptoms. There remain many countries in the world—among them the Moslem countries—where classical conversion hysterias are still extremely common and where sexuality is still highly repressed. By contrast, such disorders are much rarer in the Western world.

D. Schwartz, M. G. Thompson, and C. L. Johnson, 1982
p. 29

弖

Anorexia Is an Increasingly Common Mode of Self-Control

IT MAY BE USEFUL to view anorexia nervosa on a continuum of dieting, eating, and body-preoccupation patterns in the general population. Anorexia nervosa, rather than a rare psychiatric disorder, may represent an extreme form of an increasingly common mode of life-organization and psychological self-control in women.

Michael Thompson and Donald Schwartz, 1982
p. 49

弖

Extraordinary Time and Energy Are Devoted to Taking Off Weight

IT IS CLEAR THAT extreme consciousness of weight begins in childhood and pre-adolescence, not during teenage years. Seven-, eight-, and nine-year-olds are concerned about weight. Just as fathers may demand athletic prowess in their Little Leaguer sons, so mothers are attentive to the slightest sign of obesity in their young daughters. Many young people grow up in families where parents have pushed the same 5–15 pounds of socially undesired weight up and down the scale all of their adult lives. In upper middle-class society, an extraordinary percentage of time, energy, and psychologic activity is devoted to taking off the same slight excess of weight, which is usually repeatedly put back on. Scolding or educational notes are taped on refrigerators. Pictures of unattractive obese animals are posted around the house. Scales are placed in strategic positions. Holidays are followed by rituals of self-abasement and new, more stringent dietary plans.

Arnold Andersen, 1985
p. 30

己

Dieting Is a Major Cultural Denial of Reality

IT HAS BEEN estimated that 20 million Americans are currently on a "serious diet" for weight reduction. Ten billion dollars a year is spent on the diet industry in America, including books, health spas, diet groups, etc. This is an anomaly in human experience, where hunger and starvation haunt much of the world population. It has been viewed as a function of an affluent society–overfed, overstimulated by food, physically inactive, nutritionally unbalanced, and stressed. Truly the obsession with dieting is a national problem. More discouraging are the reports which suggest that 90–98 percent of those on "successful" weight-loss diets will regain the lost weight or more when a careful 2-to-5-year followup assessment is made. Frankly, the picture represents a major cultural denial of reality.

Janet Surrey, 1985
p. 1

己

Fat Phobia Reflects a Cultural Devaluing of the Full Development of the Adult Woman

THE PREVAILING norms and standards of what constitutes female attractiveness warrant careful examination. In many cultures, the standards of female beauty suggest the glorification of fullness, plump-ness and roundness, where the female body reflects a symbol of fertility and abundance. Our cultural norms reflect a value shift to extreme thinness, flatness, and smallness in all areas (except the bust)—a body type reflective of a preadolescent girl or young man. Perhaps we should wonder if this "fat phobia" in our society reflects a cultural debasing or devaluing of the full development of the adult woman. Perhaps the new cultural body ideals reflect the current cultural obsession with more traditionally male values—stressing linearity over fluidity, definitive ego boundaries over more perme-able and flexible boundaries, and the discomfort with, and avoidance of, certain basic human needs for nurturance and contact. The hatred of "fat" seems to reflect a cultural conflict around oral issues, issues of emotional and physical needs and dependencies.

Janet Surrey, 1985
p. 4

Fatness Was a Sign of Affluence until the Middle of This Century

U NTIL THE MIDDLE of this century, thinness was evidence of poverty, not success; and to be poor meant increased morbidity from disease, especially the infectious ones. The signs of a happy and affluent man in the nineteenth century were his paunch, his fat wife, and his chubby children. Freud (1900) describes a woman whose vomiting was an unconscious way of making herself unattractive, quite the reverse of today's woman who "fears fat."

Daniel Gesensway, 1988
p. 303

Western Society Offers Freedom that Is Frightening

LIKE MOST upper- and middle-class adolescent girls growing up into womanhood in a Western society during the last half of the twentieth century, the potential anorectic has been granted permission to use her talents, to advance her intellectual ambitions, to do everything that a human being is meant to do in the course of a lifetime. She has been given license to pursue her sexual desires in any way she sees fit with any person she deems desirable. For most girls and boys, this sudden newfound freedom is frightening, a little too much to manage, a little too soon to assimilate without considerable conflict. But erotic and moral freedom is terrifying for a best little girl whose morality before adolescence was based on absolute obedience and submissions to exacting rules and regulations.

Louise Kaplan, 1991
p. 462

The Woman Has Been Killed Off in the Anorexic

THE ANOREXIC may begin her journey defiant, but from the point of view of a male-dominated society, she ends up as the perfect woman. She is weak, sexless, and voiceless, and can only with difficulty focus on a world beyond her plate. The woman has been killed off in her. She is almost not there. Seeing her like this, unwomaned, it makes crystalline sense that a half-conscious but virulent mass movement of the imagination created the vital lie of skeletal female beauty. A future in which industrialized nations are peopled with anorexia-driven women is one of few conceivable that would save the current distribution of wealth and power from the claims made on it by women's struggle for equality.

Naomi Wolf, 1991
p. 197

Dieting Is Being Careful

W HAT IF SHE doesn't worry about her body and eats enough for all the growing she has to do? She might rip her stockings and slam-dance on a forged ID to the Pogues, and walk home barefoot, holding her shoes, alone at dawn; she might baby-sit in a battered-women's shelter one night a month; she might skateboard down Lombard Street with its seven hairpin turns, or fall in love with her best friend and do something about it, or lose herself for hours gazing into test tubes with her hair a mess, or climb a promontory with the girls and get drunk at the top, or sit down when the Pledge of Allegiance says stand, or hop a freight train, or take lovers without telling her last name, or run away to sea. She might revel in all the freedoms that seem so trivial to those who could take them for granted; she might dream seriously the dreams that seem so obvious to those who grew up with them really available. Who knows what she would do? Who knows what it would feel like?

But if she *is not careful* she will end up: raped, pregnant, impossible to control, or merely what is now called fat. The teenage girl knows this. Everyone is telling her to be careful. She learns that making her body into her landscape to tame is preferable to any kind of wildness.

Dieting is being careful, and checking into a hunger camp offers the ultimate in care.

Naomi Wolf, 1991
p. 217

Women Are Often Blocked from Achieving, Men Are Often Blocked from Doing Anything Else

A SUMMARY OF the differences in male and female socialization in our culture might go as follows. In the course of their development, boys are encouraged to ignore and transcend the currents of emotion that comprise the shared consciousness of family and community life. The development of immunity to these emotional forces is believed, undoubtedly with some justification, to permit the development of a level of objectivity that informs our most cherished social institutions, and that, by freeing males of excessive concern for the emotional needs of others, maximizes their intellectual and physical achievements. To be able to transcend feelings is largely what is meant by "being a man."

Girls, by contrast, are encouraged to be attuned to the feelings of others, to feel responsible for meeting others' emotional needs, and to create and sustain human relationships. Although a girl may be encouraged to achieve, her experience leads her to feel that an accomplishment won at the expense of others is a hollow victory. Through most of history, emotional responsiveness has been the defining characteristic of a "good woman." If the imperative to attend has created a unique set of burdens and problems for girls and women, the imperative to ignore, not to know, has created a parallel set of burdens and problems for boys and men. If females are often enslaved by interpersonal relationships, men are often excluded from them. If women are often blocked from achieving, men are often blocked from doing anything else.

Susan Wooley, 1991
p. 247

Conflict over Social Expectations Contributes to Symptom Formation

THE EXPECTATIONS and demands for sexual expression and participation have placed profound social pressure on all adolescents. In a particular group of young women with a specific neurotic (or occasionally psychotic) character structure, these demands are more than they can tolerate and symptoms make an early appearance. At puberty such external stimulation and expectation give rise to overwhelming unconscious internal conflict. In all probability, the unconscious (and to some extent conscious) guilt over drives and appetites, with their accompanying unconscious fantasies, have always caused conflicts to the adolescent in every age and every society. In the middle-class Western world, the change in attitudes and morality in the past two decades has been enormous. Outside social pressures and temptations from the media, the adult world, and the adolescent's peers are no longer under the control of the family. Conflict leading to devastating symptoms is inevitable in a group of predisposed children.

Charles Hogan, 1992
p. 112

己

The "Ideal" Body Weight Is Impossible to Achieve by Healthy Postpubertal Women

SINCE THE 1960s, with the advent of fashion model Twiggy, the fashion, entertainment, and media industries in America and her economic partners have advocated an ideal feminine image that is emaciated. Lovers of ballet will notice that, in the past two decades, the body weight of the prima ballerina has decreased continuously. While this pattern has persisted for over 25 years, it has never been acknowledged by the media that this body type is impossible to achieve by a healthy postpubertal woman. The fantastically high frequency of illness in women athletes, dancers, entertainers, and media personalities – all highly visible women – is an "open secret" that their young protégées know but do not discuss. Jane Fonda's admission that she was bulimic in the late 1980s was reported widely and greeted with shock by the media – and then buried in a series of videotapes for the exercise-obsessed.

Given that a young teenage girl must have approximately 13 percent body fat to reach menarche, in order to maintain an emaciated state (15 percent underweight or more) she will at least lose her reproductive functioning. Those who cannot deny themselves food, and purge or fast to lose weight, will deplete their bodies of electrolytes and fluid necessary for normal heart, kidney, and liver function. Despite over ten years of documentation in the popular literature that anorexia nervosa and bulimia carry a high mortality rate, it also remains an "open secret" that rapid weight loss can mean metabolic collapse and/or sudden death.

Laura Giat Roberto, 1993
p. 6

20

Suicide and Death

In Good Health Even Up to the Time of Death

STRIKING IS THEIR remarkable energy and tolerance of fatigue. Always a surprise is the fact that they are in good health during starvation, sometimes even up to the time of death.

John Sours, 1980
p. 6

From One to Ten Percent Die

ALTHOUGH DEATH does occur in starvation, the anorectic seldom seems aware of her precarious situation. Until she is engaged in treatment, she does not speak about death. And when treatment is a failure and the anorectic returns home to a hating, rejecting parent, death from starvation becomes a real possibility. From 1 to 10 percent die.

John Sours, 1980
p. 307

⊐

Family Denial Can Lead to Death

THE CLINICAL histories of those patients who had died indicated that in each instance the parent or the spouse denied the patient's emotional problem, covertly undermined treatment, and refused to take part in conjoint therapy.

John Sours, 1980
p. 313

⊐

Anger at Separation May Lead to Suicide

IT IS NOT WISE to accept an anorexic patient for therapy shortly before a vacation because there is a serious risk that she will express her unconscious anger at the separation by extreme fasting or even suicide.

C. Philip Wilson, 1983b
p. 33

⊐

Incapable of Comprehending Their Own Physical Needs

THESE PATIENTS play with death like children who think they can disappear by shamming dead. Incapable as they are of facing reality or even, as we shall see, of comprehending their own physical needs, they delude themselves into thinking that they can tamper with their bodies as they please.

Mara Selvini Palazzoli, 1988
p. 153

⊐

Weigh the Gravity of Every Case

IT IS ESSENTIAL *not* to start psychotherapy before weighing up the gravity of every case, one's own availability during moments of crisis, and such practical problems as traveling distance, and lack of financial resources.

Mara Selvini Palazzoli, 1988
p. 170

⊒

Death Can Mean the Strength to Have No Needs

I DO NOT THINK that death necessarily means the same to these patients as it does to us. I think they see it primarily as an escape from fusion. To risk death can mean having the strength to have no needs, to have an identity at last. In that sense it may mean having the space to live.

Marjorie P. Sprince, 1988
p. 81

⊒

Fantasies of Death Can Be Profoundly Undermining

AT A DEEPER level, some of the more borderline and schizophrenic-like anorexics have already secretly come to view suicide as an almost palpable transitional object. Death, through starving the unintegrated, partitioned-off body can become a profoundly undermining fantasy, designed to negate both separation and attachment and to deny feelings of abandonment.

R. Ian Story, 1990
p. 4

⊒

Each Year 150,000 American Women
Die of Anorexia

EACH YEAR, according to the [American Anorexia and Bulimia] Association, 150,000 American women die of anorexia. If so, every twelve months there are 17,024 more deaths in the United States alone than the total number of deaths from AIDS tabulated by the World Health Organization in 177 countries and territories from the beginning of the epidemic until the end of 1988; if so, more die of anorexia in the United States each year than died in ten years of civil war in Beirut.

Naomi Wolf, 1991
p. 182

⊐

Mortality

EATING DISORDERS are among the most life threatening of all psychiatric conditions. A full 8–18 percent of anorexic patients die as a result of the affliction. Because patients with pure bulimia have not been followed as long, their specific mortality rate is not known, but it appears to be less than among restricting anorexic patients. Still, electrolyte imbalance (particularly metabolic alkalosis, hypochloremia, hypokalemia, and hypomagnesemia), cardiac arrhythmias, esophageal tears, gastric rupture, and acute recurrent pancreatitis may pose life-threatening problems to the bulimic patient.

Kathryn Zerbe, 1992
p. 170

21

Symptoms

Wishes, Aims, and Conflicts Can Be
Expressed through Eating

By virtue of its connection with the earliest gratifying and frustrating experiences with the object, eating has the longest and most complex history as a modality for the expression of wishes, aims, and conflicts relating to the object. Eating can be used for the expression of conflicts over loving and being loved, loving and hating, attacking and being attacked, punishing and being punished. The connection between eating difficulties and ambivalence conflicts is thus no surprise.

Samuel Ritvo, 1980
p. 453

Symptoms May Become Part of the Sense of Identity

Meaningful treatment needs to achieve much more than restoration of the weight. I have seen endless numbers of chronic cases who had been sick and in treatment of various forms for many years. Usually there had been repeated hospitalizations to force the weight up and increasingly angry battles with doctors and families. Often the symptoms lose their dynamic significance and become nearly automatic, and patients will incorporate them in their sense of identity.

Hilde Bruch, 1982a
p. 14

Extreme Sensations of Hunger, Fullness and Activity May Be Sought

ANOTHER ASPECT of this strange behavior where the patient swings wildly from one extreme state to another may be understood in terms of seeking stimulation. Satisfaction of hunger does not suffice. It is the extreme sensations of hunger and fullness which are sought. Intensity of stimulation is a goal. In this light, we should reexamine the meaning of such typical activities long seen in the eating-disordered patient. I am referring to the hyperactivity—pacing, running, swimming long distances, exercising, and in general being unable to sit in place and simply be with oneself. This manic-like activity is not simply to lose weight, but to experience oneself intensely. I submit that the nature of this activity is self-stimulatory.

Alan Goodsitt, 1983
p. 54

The Illness Becomes the Central Organizing Event

FOR MANY, THE binge–vomit sequence provides a temporary sense of organization. The disturbing vague, amorphous feelings that preceded the binge are now replaced by intensely felt affects easily attributable to a discrete event, the binge. "I feel guilty for bingeing." "I hate myself for bingeing." Self-starvation also serves the same organizing function. "Nobody likes me because I'm fat. Therefore I have to lose weight." Everything is explained or related to the illness itself. The illness becomes the central organizing event in life. "If I give up my symptoms, what do I do?" The illness per se also substitutes for a coherently organized set of goals and values.

Alan Goodsitt, 1983
p. 55

己

Frustration Often Results in Self-starvation

EVERY ASPECT of food choice, the actual methods of eating and the weight loss are associatively linked to, and stand for, aspects of external events that are out of control. When patients cannot achieve what they wish with their friends and family, and with their hopes and aspirations, they act out with food. A frustration in the external world, such as an argument with a parent, often results in an exacerbation of the self-starvation.

Ira Mintz, 1983c
p. 91

己

There Is Moral Relief in Starvation and Vomiting

SELF-STARVATION is a wonderful antidote for guilt and reparation — witness Lent and Yom Kippur and the taboo foods of other cultures. So is purgation; the vomiting and exercise of the bulimic is not solely to evacuate calories; they are a means of disgorging guilt. Guilt is not merely a bad feeling of feeling bad; it is a physical experience of an almost ineradicable tension. Physical means are accordingly required to expunge the feeling. There is moral relief in violent exercise, exhaustive defecation and vomiting. There is even a kind of moral sensuality in the experience of "bingeing," when the glut of gluttony is reached.

Harold Boris, 1984a
p. 438

己

Hunger Itself Serves as the Anodyne for Loneliness

HUNGER IS UNDENIABLE and durable. At sufficient levels of intensity it makes one oblivious of everything else. (Accounts by people who were in concentration camps give poignant testimony of this.) For the anorectic that means everything else is obliterated. If they are not obliterated by hunger itself filling the furthest reaches of the mind, they are obliterated by the experience of eating—bingeing—and then by mortification of the spirit or, via diuretics, laxatives or vomiting or compulsive exercise, of the flesh. For people of a different stripe, eating consoles loneliness: for the anorectic it is precisely hunger itself that paradoxically serves as the anodyne for loneliness.

Harold Boris, 1984b
p. 319

己

Substance Abuse Is Sometimes Present

A SMALL BUT important group of bulimic patients, less than 20 percent of those entering our clinic, also have significant substance abuse problems, usually alcohol or cocaine abuse. The coexistence of these problems requires urgent attention, often taking priority over the bulimic symptoms alone.

Joel Yager, 1985
p. 207

己

Symptoms May Serve to Sustain an
Attachment at a Distance

EATING-DISORDERED individuals are often quite distrustful of signifi-cant others. They have considerable difficulty sharing the details of personal experiences fearing that no one will be available for them and that they will only be opening themselves up for attack. Moreover, separations such as the end of a therapy session or a vacation may further reinforce patients' beliefs regarding the nonviability of long-term intimate relationships. Disturbances in attachment are also functionally associated with specific eating-disorder behaviors. We suspect that for some individuals, restrictively dieting provides a means of sustaining an attachment, at a safe distance, without acknowledging this need. Bingeing may fill an emptiness for nurturance and may be a mechanism for self-soothing for individuals who cannot trust that an intimate relationship with significant others can meet these same needs.

Judith Armstrong and David Roth, 1989
p. 153

己

Women Tend to Use Food in the Service of Defense; Men Tend to Use Alcohol Abuse and Sexualization

A LARGE PROPORTION of my female patients, far more extensively than my male patients, tend to use food directly in the service of defense (i.e., repression, denial, and/or displacement) against primitive types of anxiety around dependency, either in combination with other defenses or in a more isolated way. This acting out usually takes the form of overeating, but sometimes undereating or a combination of both. A similar proportion of my male patients appear to employ intermittent alcohol abuse and sexualization in the service of defense against similar types of anxiety. These behaviors may be utilized separately, together or in combination with other defenses. Intermittent drug use and tobacco smoking seem to be less gender-related as I find, and colleagues concur, that they are employed by members of both sexes in comparable proportions.

Laura Arens Fuerstein, 1989
p. 165

⊐

The Layering of Meanings Is an Essential
Aspect of the Symptoms

THE QUEST FOR A solitary underlying meaning is only one approach to the problem. It assumes that the mystery has one solution, one basic hidden truth, and narrows the science of interpretation to an unveiling of this basic truth. Sometimes this approach makes sense in the diagnostic interpretation of medical symptoms and signs. Unfortunately, the search for an ultimate meaning denies the complexity of the psychiatric symptom. In confronting the inevitable competition of different contexts and interpretations we need to ask whether the function of a symptom might not be precisely to weave together diverse contexts into a single metaphorical fabric. By defering the search for one correct interpretation and instead examining the relationship among several meanings of a symptom we might learn more about the symptom's capacity to integrate aspects of the patient's world. The layering of meanings may be an essential aspect of the symptom-sign, only obscured by our own need for simplification, explanation, and certainty. If the goal shifts from a search for the single true meaning of the symptom to a description of multiple meanings and contexts, the task becomes finding a way to look at a complex phenomenon without succumbing to a sense of chaos.

Paul Hamburg, 1989
p. 132

⊐

A Strong Internal Force Fears the Loss of Symptoms

EVERY DEMAND for freedom from psychological symptoms is a paradoxical one, in that these symptoms are childlike attempts at self-cure and were created as a solution to unbearable mental pain. There is, therefore, a strong internal force that fears the loss of symptoms in spite of the suffering they cause; this will tend to create considerable resistance to the analytic process.

Joyce McDougall, 1989
p. 8

己

Even Affects of Pleasure May Mobilize the Craving for the Addictive Object

THE PARADOX presented by the addictive object is that, in spite of its sometimes death-dealing potential, it is always invested as a good object by some part of the mind. Whatever the object may be, it is inevitably endowed with the supreme quality of enabling the addicted person to rapidly dispel mental conflict and psychic pain, even if only briefly. In the same vein, we can understand why even affects of pleasure may mobilize the craving for the addictive object in these analysands, just as a small child in states of excitement needs its mother to act as a protective and filtering screen against emotional flooding. However, the soothing substance has to be sought ceaselessly in the external world, usually in increasing quantities.

Joyce McDougall, 1989
p. 97

己

Gorging and Vomiting Can Be Used to Banish Unpleasant Feelings

SARA CAME TO AN hour one day and said she noted that when she was alone and didn't want to be and no one was available to her, she felt lonely and empty. These were first psychological feeling states but then the emptiness became a body state, more than a feeling state, and she coped with that by gorging, which relieved the feeling of emptiness. She then vomited so as not to gain weight. In addition, it became clear that gorging and vomiting could be applied nonspecifically to rid herself of any unpleasant feeling or thought or body state. So, whenever she felt bad, whenever she had thoughts she didn't like, for example, obsessions that she couldn't banish in any other way, or whenever she was caught up in compulsive behavior she couldn't interrupt in any other way, she would gorge and then vomit, and afterwards felt better.

Along these same lines, she noted that at some point she had stopped feeling bad in the sense of feeling anxious or depressed and, instead of feeling those feelings, what she felt was fat! Given this situation, the understandable solution to bad feelings, now experienced as a feeling of fatness, was to lose ever more weight. After doing so, she felt better; the mechanism worked. In addition, it was under her control in a very reliable and predictable manner. Thus, over time, maintenance of feeling states had shifted to maintenance of a body state, primarily body weight, and the locus of activity shifted from the interpersonal and intrapsychic fields, the ordinary sources of good feeling states, to the mind–body field.

As this was being clarified, I told her I thought successful treatment would involve reversing that process. It would have to be done slowly, in manageable doses, but I thought it was very important for her to get back to a state of affairs where, if she felt anxious, she felt anxious and not fat, and then found some new solution to managing her anxiety.

James Sacksteder, 1989a
p. 414

Weight Loss as a Way of Becoming Free of All Problems

PATTY'S RELATIONSHIP to her body was . . . tyrannical, punishing, and sadistic. Weight reduction became her way of trying to free herself of all her troubles. With sufficient weight loss, she no longer had menstrual periods or sexual feelings, thus she no longer missed men and didn't long for the possibility of a good relationship with one. Weight loss brought self-respect and a fleeting feeling of contentment, satisfaction, and accomplishment. Any weight gain, on the other hand, or simply the failure to lose ever more weight, brought pain, a feeling of helplessness and despair, and a feeling of being totally out of control not just of her weight but of her body and all its functions, her mind, her feelings, her relationships with people, everything. She felt a humiliating, devastating failure. Peace could be reestablished only with renewed and again successful efforts to lose yet more weight. Her life had essentially shrunk to the two-person field of her psyche and her soma. No one else was very relevant.

James Sacksteder, 1989b
p. 389

己

Unrealistic for the Therapist to Expect the Patient to Give Up Symptoms Before There Are Alternatives

A FREQUENT UNREALISTIC expectation by the therapist concerns the actual eating symptoms. As destructive as an eating disorder can be, eating symptoms, nonetheless, are usually helpful to, or do something for, the individual. If not, eating disorders would not be so prevalent nor as resistant to treatment. It must be assumed that the eating disorder represents the best adjustment the individual can make. Thus, it is unrealistic for the therapist to expect the patient to give up symptoms before helping replace them with alternatives that work as well.

Ron A. Thompson and Roberta T. Sherman, 1989
p. 63

己

The Body Can Be Used as a Fetish

STARVING THE BODY and self-induced vomiting take on, for many anorexics, qualities of dependable fetishes that are more reliable than any other tie, animate or otherwise. The body of the self-flogging, starving patient becomes very nearly like a fetishistic object to her as she attempts to differentiate and elevate self and bodily controls to a state of perfect detachment. In treating her body and anorexic rituals fetishistically rather than as useful transitional objects or experiences, she learns that this approach produces extremely self-soothing and anxiety-regulating results, however short-lived. She finds, as the therapist also soon will or needs to find, that anorexia nervosa unhappily works only too well in terms of attaining control and predictability. The anorexic discovers that she can depend on her body, on this thing that is all hers—although many understandably complain that they don't feel it or know where their bodies begin and end—and which she can usually rely on, more or less predict, and bring under her Olympian powers of control and defensive dissociation.

R. Ian Story, 1990
p. 4

ᄅ

The Symptom Is a Condensed Version of the Patient's Developmental Drama

FROM A PSYCHOANALYTIC perspective, symptomatic behavior is an effort to integrate the present with the unconscious past. The eating disorder symptom is an indirect response to a developmental problem, a final common pathway for psychological conflict. Hence, even though the symptomatic behavior may disappear (temporarily or permanently), the underlying problematic dynamics remain until they are addressed. The diagnosis must be made on the basis of the person's dynamics, internal object relations, and early development, all of which predate the symptom and, in some cases, remain after the symptom has ceased.

Broadly speaking, the eating disorder symptom is an expression of unconscious conflict. Within the context of treatment, it may become a desperate personal communication about the patient's fears, wishes, and fantasies presented in condensed form. It communicates what the patient has experienced but cannot express. In it is contained a fragmentary version of the patient's developmental and historical drama—a narrative in its most condensed form, containing the wish and also the fear. As in all addiction symptoms, its repetitive quality both results in and evidences a sense of hopelessness and despair.

John Schneider, 1991
p. 197

〓

Numerous Conflicts Can Be Expressed by the Symptoms of Gorging and Purging

NUMEROUS UNCONSCIOUS conflicts can be expressed via the gorging and purging of the bulimic syndrome. Sadomasochistic conflicts, for example, are expressed, in regard to the torture of the body, which is equated with the maternal representation; the control that is attempted over the body has a sadistic quality. The misguided attempt to keep the body slim can be an attempt by such a woman to maintain a masculine body self, which can then compete with men for the sexual love of the mother. Dependent conflicts can be expressed via the bingeing, while hostile repudiation and an attempt to maintain autonomy can be expressed through purging. In those occasional borderline bulimics, the alternating between bingeing and purging may even serve to maintain the self–other boundary. Finally, struggles with narcissistic equilibrium can be expressed via the body self. An emphasis on the ideal body self and the bulimic adolescent's struggles to attain it can help her to avoid the more profound sense of despair and inadequacy associated with her defensively distorted, preoedipal idealization of her mother. Failures to attain this ideal can be circumscribed, so that a more encompassing sense of self-criticism and failure is avoided. In this way, the discrepancy between the ideal self-representation and the actual self-representation can be minimized.

Alan Sugarman, 1991
p. 13

〓

The Unconscious Role of Exercise May Be to
Discharge Aggression

WHILE EXERCISE HAS been recognized as an integral component of the anorexic-bulimic syndrome, it has usually been viewed as a conscious means of regulating weight levels and of controlling the individual's fear of being fat. Its unconscious role of mediating aggressive drive discharge and increased ego control over a component of the environment has been minimized. From this perspective, we can consider that different types of exercise, especially running, can serve to drain off intolerable levels of aggressive build-up and attempt to reestablish more acceptable levels of ego homeostasis, preventing overt anorexic decompensation.

Ira Mintz, 1992a
p. 358

Physical Complications of Anorexia Nervosa

PHYSICAL COMPLICATIONS of anorexia nervosa include all serious sequelae of malnutrition, including cardiovascular compromise. Prepubertal patients may have arrested sexual maturation, general physical development, and growth and may not grow to anticipated heights. Even patients who look and feel deceptively well and who have normal ECGs often have bradycardia and other manifestations of impaired cardiac function, such as drop in orthostatic blood pressure and increase in pulse rate, and may be prone to sudden death. Prolonged amenorrhea (more than 6 months) is associated with potentially irreversible osteopenia and a correspondingly higher rate of pathological fractures. Patients may suffer from dehydration, electrolyte disturbances, gastrointestinal motility disturbances, infertility, hypothermia and other evidence of hypometabolism, and from the psychological sequelae of starvation.

American Psychiatric Association, 1993
p. 213

⊒

Physical Complications of Bulimic Behaviors

Physical complications of bulimic behaviors include electrolyte disturbances (notably, a hypokalemic, hypochloremic alkalosis in patients who vomit), mineral and fluid imbalances, hypomagnesemia, gatric and esophageal irritation and bleeding, large bowel abormalities due to laxative abuse, erosion of dental enamel, parotid enlargement, and accompanying hyperamylasemia. Mallory-Weiss esophageal tears occur rarely. Abuse of ipecac to induce vomiting may cause cardio-myopathies (with sudden death) or peripheral muscle weakness.

American Psychiatric Association, 1993
p. 213

22

Transference

Determined to Discourage or Exasperate the Therapist

Patients suffering from anorexia nervosa are easily identified, even on first acquaintance: their attitude to the therapist, to whom they are often brought by members of their family against their will, is generally studied, cold and forbidding, though quite a few are fatuous, loquacious, hypocritical and inconsistent. But no matter what particular stance they adopt, all alike seem determined to discourage or exasperate the physician. They all insist that they are perfectly well and appear to be completely unconcerned about their grave physical condition or their amenorrhea.

Mara Selvini Palazzoli, 1963
p. 18

⊐

Fear Underlies Passivity

Anorexia nervosa patients have no love for the therapist, who, in turn, finds it hard to respond with sympathy. At first their attitude is

237

rarely aggressive or openly scornful; it is merely cold and passive. However, their frigidity is simply a screen for their acute fears and suspicions and for their determination to ward off all approaches.

Mara Selvini Palazzoli, 1963
p. 111

Defended against Dependent Feelings

T HE CONSTANT ready availability of their own bodies for the representation and expression of psychic conflict made it more difficult to bring the conflicts into the transference, a difficulty compounded by the need to defend against the dependent feelings in the transference and against the rage at the analyst when these dependent wishes and needs could not be gratified.

Samuel Ritvo, 1980
p. 455

Compliance Is Repeated in the Transference

T HE TRAITS THAT develop from the necessity to be so accommodating and compliant are transferred into treatment. As children these patients became practically mind readers who were exceedingly sensitive to what they felt the grownups wanted. They were also convinced that their mothers always knew how and what they felt. In therapy they are disappointed, after an initial period of overadmiration (or the opposite, indiscriminate negativism), when their expectation that the therapist should understand what they feel and are going through, without their putting it into words, is not fulfilled. The unrealistic aspects of their feeling that "mother always knew what I felt" need to be reexamined—that in fact the opposite was true and mother often disregarded their feelings, and that it is the task of therapy to help them discover their own needs and values. Thus they can come to the

point of trusting their own decisions and respecting their own opin-
ions instead of being overpowered by the judgment of others. By being
tuned in to the slightest distortion in their sense of reality the therapist
can instigate, without being judgmental, necessary reevaluations.

Hilde Bruch, 1982b
p. 1537

己

Demanding Yet Fearful of Assertion

IN THE TRANSFERENCE, anorexic patients become demanding, manipulative, and hostile in an attempt to control and coerce the therapist
into backing down, just as they felt forced to behave over the years by
the controlling parent. Concomitantly, however, in identifying with
the weak, helpless aspects of their own personality, they are fearful of
retaliation by the therapist for their assertiveness, thus anticipating a
response similar to that of the parent. These attitudes must be revealed
and discussed carefully as transference manifestations.

Ira Mintz, 1983c
p. 98

己

Yearning to Be Held, Touched and
Ultimately Merged

THE DESPERATE search for alleviation of unbearable affects becomes
an all-consuming preoccupation, expressed in the transference as a
yearning to be held, touched, fed and ultimately merged with the
object. . . . But the very union that is sought so tenaciously brings
with it a sense of primitive fury, leading to threats of invasion, mutual
destruction and disintegration. Only by creating a distance from the
real object and replacing it by a concrete controllable substitute can
the terror be averted. Thus the preoccupation with the object, its
comforts and dangers, is replaced by a consuming preoccupation with

the comforts and dangers of food. Food now replaces the missing part of the self while it is employed at the same time to maintain the boundaries between self and non-self.

Marjorie Sprince, 1984
p. 200

Fear that Open Expression of Anger and Envy Would Destroy the Therapist/Mother

A MAJOR RISK IN treatment is that the patient will unwittingly manipulate the therapist into playing the mother's part as she experienced it, that is, by being alternately intrusive and rejecting, thus confirming her worst fears about the hazards of separation and independence. If the therapist's well-meant efforts to impose structure and foster self-control are both requested and repeatedly resisted then she/he may easily feel discouraged and exasperated. These misguided attempts at autonomy by the patient may even in extreme cases provoke the therapist's withdrawal or termination of treatment. Paradoxically, it may feel safer for the patient to induce such a rejection than to risk any open expression of her anger, resentment, and envy which, if unleashed, would destroy the therapist/mother.

Hilary J. Beattie, 1988
p. 458

Reworks the Struggle with Mother in the Relationship with the Therapist

IT IS ALSO VITAL to interpret and gradually bring to consciousness the central, underlying conflict with the mother and the patient's fears that any change or improvement will lead to devastating separation and loss. Many of these patients have defensively idealized or distanced their mothers and are terrified of recognizing their own neediness and hostility towards them, although they act it out daily in their eating patterns and also in their interactions with the therapist. As treatment proceeds and the original conflict surfaces, it may eventually become possible for the patient to admit and tolerate it and thereby gradually rework the struggle in the relationship with the therapist.

Hilary J. Beattie, 1988
p. 458

⊒

Escape into Physical Symptoms to Avoid a Relationship with the Therapist

SOME OF THE gravest cases will often show a marked deterioration to avoid falling into what to them is the fatal trap of an interpersonal relationship with the therapist: because they feel irresistably drawn into the transference situation, escape into physical symptoms is their only means of preserving their autonomy and their relative independence from what, as experience has taught them, is bound to prove yet another symbiotic and destructive relationship.

Mara Selvini Palazzoli, 1988
p. 168

⊒

They Are Terrified of Intimate Relationships

THEY MUST BE treated with extreme patience and sympathy. Because of their fragile personalities, they are terrified of any kind of intimate interpersonal relationship for which they nevertheless long with passion. With them the therapist must expect constant demands for a reduction in the number of weekly sessions, repeated absences justified in the most childish manner, or requests for a temporary interruption of the treatment.

Mara Selvini Palazzoli, 1988
p. 168

Devaluing the Therapist Can Mask Idealizing Needs

W E NEED ALSO to recognize that our patients' devaluations of us often mask idealizing needs—idealizing needs which the patient is afraid to express for fear that the longed-for idealized other will disappoint her now as in the past. We must also be aware of how our patients' thwarted need for a soothing, idealized merger may have led to its apparent opposite—a false and brittle "independence." With these precociously independent patients, we need to encourage attachment and dependency through interpretation of our patients' fears of what will happen to them should they allow the therapist to become important to them.

Susan Sands, 1989
p. 100

The Unfolding of Resistance and Transference

A T THE START OF each session, Jessica always chose the chair most physically distant from me. Her eyes were constantly averted, as if eye-to-eye contact was excruciatingly painful. As the therapy unfolded, it became clear that her eye aversion had multiple meanings. Initially, it appeared to be simply an identification with other family members, particularly her father, who habitually avoided or minimized eye contact. Further inquiry revealed that it was reflective of her profound sense of shame: Jessica experienced herself as so wanting in so many domains that she literally preferred not to be seen. At a deeper level, reconstruction suggested that the eye aversion was an attempt to avoid a traumatic recapitulation of her early relationship with her mother. This was disclosed in the context of the transference relationship, when she told me that to make eye contact was to become imprisoned by me. By this she meant that she would be compelled to "cue off" me; to read my facial expressions for signs of, say, approval or disapproval; to assess my body postures to see whether I was interested or uninterested—in short, to compulsively *react* to me. By avoiding eye contact, Jessica believed that at least she had the hope of being free, of being herself, of *acting* instead of *reacting* for the first time in her life. This transference attitude was eventually linked to early failures in the process of separation-individuation from her mother through the mode of repeated interpretation and working through. From transference material we were able to reconstruct together her earliest perceptions of her hyperemotional mother as an intrusive, dominating, and needy caretaker. In order to ensure the survival of the relationship, she had to march to her mother's beat. Too much independence ran the risk of maternal withdrawal and abandonment.

Silence was the major manifestation of resistance in the first part of psychotherapy. Jessica had great difficulty with the idea and practice of free association. In a flash of insight she stated, "I am used to saying what I *should* say, but I have no idea of what I *want* to say." Nonetheless, silence pervaded many of the early sessions. Beneath her silence raged an internal struggle between holding back and keeping secret versus letting go and sharing, reminiscent of a toddler struggling fiercely with anal issues. To Jessica's categorical way of thinking, to share just a little was equivalent to "total vulnerability," and the terrifying self-perception that she was becoming a "giant liquefying Jell-O," without boundaries or definition. In contrast, keeping secret and silent meant security, but at the exorbitant cost of utter emotional isolation.

With further work it also became evident that her silence had enormous transference implications. We were able to clarify that Jessica feared that if she shared deeper parts of herself, I would be silently contemptuous and disapproving. This was linked to present and past perceptions of her aloof, methodical father.

William James Swift, 1991
p. 58

References

Altshuler, K. Z., and Weiner, M. F. (1985). Anorexia nervosa and depression: a dissenting view. *American Journal of Psychiatry* 142: 328–332.

American Psychiatric Association (1980). *Diagnostic and Statistical Manual of Mental Disorders* (3rd ed.). Washington, DC: American Psychiatric Association.

_____ (1993). Practice guidelines for eating disorders. *American Journal of Psychiatry* 150:2, 212–228.

Andersen, A. E. (1985). *Practical Comprehensive Treatment of Anorexia Nervosa and Bulimia.* Baltimore: Johns Hopkins University Press.

_____ (1990). Males with eating disorders. *Eating Disorders Monograph Series.* New York: Brunner/Mazel.

Andersen, A. E., and Mickalide, A. D. (1983). Anorexia nervosa in the male: an underdiagnosed disorder. *Psychosomatics* 24: 1066–1075.

Armstrong, J. G., and Roth, D. M. (1989). Attachment and separation difficulties in eating disorders: a preliminary investigation. *International Journal of Eating Disorders* 8:141–155.

Aronson, J. K. (1986). The level of object relations and severity of symptoms in the normal weight bulimic patient. *International Journal of Eating Disorders* 5:669–681.

Barth, D. (1988). The treatment of bulimia from a self psychological perspective. *Clinical Social Work Journal* 15:270–281.

_____ (1991). When the patient abuses food. In *Using Self Psychology in Psychotherapy*, ed. H. Jackson. Northvale, NJ: Jason Aronson.

Barth, D., and Wurman, V. (1986). Group therapy with women: a self-psychological approach. *International Journal of Eating Disorders* 5:735–745.

Beattie, H. J. (1988). Eating disorders and the mother–daughter relationship. *International Journal of Eating Disorders* 7:453–460.

Beaumont, P. J. V., George, G. C. W., and Smart, D. E. (1976). "Dieters" and "vomiters" and "purgers" in anorexia nervosa. *Psychological Medicine* 6:617–622.

Bell, R. M. (1985). *Holy Anorexia*. Chicago: The University of Chicago Press.

Bemis, K. (1978). Current approaches to the etiology and treatment of anorexia nervosa. *Psychological Bulletin* 85:593–617.

Bemporad, J. R., and Ratey, J. (1985). Intensive psychotherapy of former anorexic individuals. *American Journal of Psychotherapy* 34:454–466.

Benedek, T. (1934). Dominant ideas and their relation to morbid cravings. Paper presented at the Thirteenth International Psycho-Analytical Congress, Lucerne, August.

Benson, A., and Futterman, L. (1985). Psychotherapeutic partnering: an approach to the treatment of anorexia and bulimia. In *Theory and Treatment of Anorexia Nervosa and Bulimia*, ed. S. W. Emmett. New York: Brunner/Mazel.

Beresin, E. V., Gordon, C., and Herzog, D. B. (1989). The process of recovering from anorexia nervosa. In *Psychoanalysis and Eating Disorders*, ed. J. R. Bemporad and D. B. Herzog. New York: Guilford.

Bergmann, M. V. (1988). On eating disorders and work inhibition. In *Bulimia: Psychoanalytic Treatment and Theory*, ed. H. J. Schwartz. Madison, CT: International Universities Press.

Birksted-Breen, D. (1989). Working with an anorexic patient. *International Journal of Psycho-Analysis* 70:29–40.

Boris, H. N. (1984a). On the treatment of anorexia nervosa. *International Journal of Psycho-Analysis* 65:435–442.

_____ (1984b). The problem of anorexia nervosa. *International Journal of Psycho-Analysis* 65:315–321.

Bram, S., Eger, D., and Halmi, K. A. (1982). Anorexia nervosa and personality type: a preliminary report. *International Journal of Eating Disorders* 2:67–74.

Brenner, D. (1983). Self regulatory functions in bulimia. *Contemporary Psychotherapy Review* 1:79–96.

_____ (1984). Anorexia-bulimia-obesity: a continuum? Paper presented at the First International Conference on Eating Disorders, New York City, April.

Brenner-Liss, D. (1986). Bulimia: a self-psychological and ego-developmental view. *American Mental Health Counselors Association Journal* 8:211–220.

Browning, W. N. (1985). Long-term dynamic group therapy with bulimic patients: a clinical discussion. In *Theory and Treatment of Anorexia and Bulimia: Biomedical, Sociocultural, and Psychological Perspectives*, ed. S. W. Emmet. New York: Brunner/Mazel.

Bruch, H. (1962). Perceptual and conceptual disturbances in anorexia nervosa. *Psychosomatic Medicine* 24:187–199.

_____ (1973). *Eating Disorders, Obesity, Anorexia Nervosa and the Person Within.* New York: Basic Books.

_____ (1977). Psychotherapy in eating disorders. *Canadian Psychiatric Association Journal* 22:102–108.

_____ (1978). *The Golden Cage: The Enigma of Anorexia Nervosa.* Cambridge, MA: Harvard University Press.

_____ (1980). Developmental deviations in anorexia nervosa. *Israel Annals of Psychiatry and Related Disciplines* 17:255–261.

_____ (1982a). Psychotherapy in anorexia nervosa. *International Journal of Eating Disorders* 1:(4)3–14.

_____ (1982b). Anorexia nervosa: therapy and theory. *The American Journal of Psychiatry* 139:1531–1538.

_____ (1988). *Conversations with Anorexics.* New York: Basic Books.

Burke, N. (1991). Starved for words: on the anorexia of language. *Psychoanalytic Psychology* 8:149–167. Hillsdale, NJ: Lawrence Erlbaum.

Byrne, K. (1987). *A Parent's Guide to Anorexia and Bulimia: Understanding and Helping Self-Starvers and Binge/Purgers.* New York: Schocken.

Carlat, D. J., and Camargo, C. A., Jr. (1991). Review of bulimia nervosa in males. *American Journal of Psychiatry* 148:831–843.

Casper, R. C. (1983). On the emergence of bulimia nervosa as a syndrome: a historical view. *International Journal of Eating Disorders* 2:3–16.

Casper, R. C., Eckert, E. D., and Halmi, K. A. (1980). Bulimia: its incidence and clinical importance in patients with anorexia nervosa. *Archives of General Psychiatry* 37:1030–1035.

Ceasar, M. (1977). The role of maternal identification in four cases of anorexia nervosa. *Bulletin of the Menninger Clinic* 41:475–486.

Charone, J. K. (1982). Eating disorders: their genesis in the mother–infant relationship. *International Journal of Eating Disorders* 1:(4)15–42.

Chatoor, I., Egan, J., Getson, P., et al. (1987). Mother–infant interactions in infantile anorexia nervosa. *Journal of the American Academy of Child and Adolescent Psychiatry* 27:535–540.

Chernin, K. (1981). *The Obsession: Reflections on the Tyranny of Slenderness.* New York: Harper & Row.

Cohler, B. J. (1977). The significance of the therapist's feelings in the treatment of anorexia nervosa. In *Adolescent Psychiatry* (vol. 5):352–384. Northvale, NJ: Jason Aronson.

Crisp, A. H. (1980). *Anorexia Nervosa: Let Me Be.* New York: Grune & Stratton.

Czyzewski, D., and Suhur, M. A., eds. (1988). *Hilde Bruch: Conversations with Anorexics.* New York: Basic Books.

Dennis, A. B., and Sansone, R. A. (1991). The clinical stages of treatment for the eating disorder patient with borderline personality disorder. In *Psychodynamic Treatment of Anorexia Nervosa and Bulimia,* ed. C. Johnson. New York: Guilford.

de Zwaan, M., and Mitchell, J. E. (1993). Medical complications of anorexia nervosa and bulimia. In *Medical Issues and the Eating Disorders: The Interface,* ed. A. S. Kaplan and P. E. Garfinkel, pp. 65–67. Eating Disorders Monograph Series No. 7. New York: Brunner/Mazel.

Eckert, E. D., Goldberg, S. C., Halmi, K. A., et al. (1979). Alcoholism in anorexia nervosa. In *Psychiatric Factors in Drug Abuse,* ed. R. Pickens and L. Heston. San Francisco: Grune & Stratton.

Fairburn, G. C. (1980). Self-induced vomiting. *Journal of Psychosomatic Research* 24:193–197.

Falstein, E. I., Sherman, D., Feinstein, S. C., and Judas, I. (1956). Anorexia nervosa in the male child. *American Journal of Orthopsychiatry* 26:751–772.

Fischer, N. (1989). Anorexia nervosa and unresolved rapprochement conflicts: a case study. *International Journal of Psycho-Analysis* 70:41–54.

Flarsheim, A. (1975). The therapist's collusion with the patient's wish for suicide. In *Tactics and Techniques in Psychoanalytic Therapy,* vol. 2, ed. P. L. Giovacchini. New York: Jason Aronson.

Forchheimer, F. (1907). Anorexia nervosa in children. *Archives of Pediatrics* 24:801–812.

Freud, A. (1946). The psychoanalytic study of infantile feeding disturbances. *Psychoanalytic Study of the Child* 2:119–131. New York: International Universities Press.

Friedman, M. (1985). Survivor guilt in the pathogenesis of anorexia nervosa. *Psychiatry* 48:25–39.

Fuerstein, L. A. (1989). Some hypotheses about gender differences in coping with oral dependency conflicts. *Psychoanalytic Review* 76: 163–184.

Garfinkel, P. E., and Garner, D. M. (1982). *Anorexia Nervosa: A Multidimensional Perspective.* New York: Brunner/Mazel.

Garfinkel, P. E., Moldofsky, H. and Garner, D. M. (1977). Prognosis in anorexia nervosa as influenced by clinical features, treatment, and self-perception. *Canadian Medical Association Journal* 117: 1041–1045.

_____ (1980). The heterogeneity of anorexia nervosa: bulimia as a distinct subgroup. *Archives of General Psychiatry* 38:1036–1040.

Garner, D. M., Garfinkel, P. E., and Bemis, K. M. (1982). A multidimensional psychotherapy for anorexia nervosa. *International Journal of Eating Disorders* 1:3–47.

Garner, D. M., Garfinkel, P. E., Schwartz, D., and Thompson, M. (1980). Cultural expectations of thinness in women. *Psychological Reports* 47:483–491.

Geist, R. A. (1984). Therapeutic dilemmas in the treatment of anorexia nervosa. *Contemporary Psychotherapy Review,* Fall.

_____ (1985). Therapeutic dilemmas in the treatment of anorexia nervosa: a self-psychological perspective. In *Theory and Treatment of Anorexia Nervosa and Bulimia: Biomedical, Sociocultural and Psychological Perspectives,* ed. S. W. Emmett. New York: Brunner/Mazel.

_____ , ed. (1989). Self psychological reflections on the origins of eating disorders. In *Psychoanalysis and Eating Disorders*, ed. J. R. Bemporad and D. B. Herzog. New York: Guilford.

Gesensway, D. (1988). A psychoanalytic study of bulimia and pregnancy. In *Bulimia: Psychoanalytic Treatment and Theory*, ed. H. Schwartz. Madison, CT: International Universities Press.

Gitlin, M. J. (1990). *The Psychotherapist's Guide to Psychopharmacology.* New York: The Free Press.

Goldman, H. E. (1988). Does she deserve to live? A psychodynamic case study of an anorexic mother and her young child. *International Journal of Eating Disorders* 7:561–566.

Gonzalez, R. (1988). Bulimia and adolescence: individual adolescent treatment. In *Bulimia: Psychoanalytic Treatment and Theory*, ed. H. Schwartz. Madison, CT: International Universities Press.

Goodsitt, A. (1983). Self-regulatory disturbances in eating disorders. *International Journal of Eating Disorders* 2:51–60.

Gordon, C., Beresin, E., and Herzog, D. B. (1989). The parents' relationship and the child's illness in anorexia nervosa. In *Psychoanalysis and Eating Disorders*, ed. J. R. Bemporad and D. B. Herzog. New York: Guilford.

Gull, W. W. (1874). Anorexia nervosa (eupepsia hysterica, anorexia hysterica). *Transactions of the Clinical Society of London* 7:22–28.

Hall, A. (1985). Group psychotherapy for anorexia nervosa. In *Handbook of Psychotherapy for Anorexia Nervosa and Bulimia*, ed. D. M. Gardner and P. E. Garfinkel. New York: Guilford.

Halmi, K. (1974). Anorexia nervosa: demographic and clinical features in 94 cases. *Psychosomatic Medicine* 36:18–25.

Halmi, K., Falk, J., and Schwartz, E. (1981). Binge-eating and vomiting: a survey of college population. *Psychological Medicine* 11:697–706.

Hamburg, P. (1989). Bulimia: the construction of a symptom. In *Psychoanalysis and Eating Disorders*, ed. J. R. Bemporad and D. B. Herzog. New York: Guilford.

Hatsukami, D., Owen, P., Pyle, R., and Mitchell, J. (1982). Similarities and differences on the MMPI between women with bulimia and women with alcohol or drug abuse problems. *Addictive Behaviors* 7:435–439.

Hawkins, R. C., and Clement, P. F. (1980). Development and construct validation of a self-report measure of binge eating tendencies. *Addictive Behaviors* 5:219–226.

Herzog, D. (1982). Bulimia: the secretive syndrome. *Psychosomatics* 23:481–487.

Herzog, D., Norman, D., Gordon, C., and Pepose, M. (1984). Sexual conflict and eating disorders in twenty seven males. *American Journal of Psychiatry* 141:989–990.

Hiltmann, H., and Clauser, G. (1961). Psychodiagnostik und aktiva-nalytische psychotherapie. *Praxis der Psychotherapy* 6:168. (Quoted in *Self-Starvation*, by M. S. Palazzoli. New York: Jason Aronson.)

Hogan, C. (1983a). Psychodynamics. In *Fear of Being Fat: The Treatment of Anorexia Nervosa and Bulimia*, ed. C. P. Wilson, C. Hogan, and I. Mintz. New York: Jason Aronson.

_____ (1983b). Transference. In *Fear of Being Fat: The Treatment of Anorexia Nervosa and Bulimia*, ed. C. P. Wilson, C. Hogan, and I. Mintz. New York: Jason Aronson.

_____ (1983c). Technical problems in psychoanalytic treatment. In *Fear of Being Fat: The Treatment of Anorexia Nervosa and Bulimia*, ed. C. P. Wilson, C. Hogan, and I. Mintz. New York: Jason Aronson.

_____ (1992). The adolescent crisis in anorexia nervosa. In *Psychodynamic Technique in the Treatment of the Eating Disorders*, ed. C. P. Wilson, C. Hogan, and I. Mintz. Northvale, NJ: Jason Aronson.

Holmgren, G., Humble, K., Norring, C., et al. (1983). The anorectic bulimic conflict and alternative diagnostic approach to anorexia nervosa and bulimia. *International Journal of Eating Disorders* 3:3–14.

Hudson, J. I., Harrison, G. P., Jr., and Jonas, J. M. (1984). Psychosis in anorexia nervosa and bulimia. *British Journal of Psychiatry* 145:420–423.

Humphrey, L. L. (1986). Family dynamics in bulimia. *Annals of Adolescent Psychiatry*, ed. S. C. Feinstein, A. H. Esman, J. G. Tooney, et al. Chicago: University of Chicago Press.

_____ (1991). Object relations and the family system: an integrative approach to understanding and treating eating disorders. In *Psychodynamic Treatment of Anorexia Nervosa and Bulimia*, ed. C. Johnson. New York: Guilford.

Janet, P. (1903). *Les Obsessions et la Psychosthenie*. Paris: Alcan.

_____ (1907). *The Major Symptoms of Hysteria*. London: Macmillan.

Johnson, C. L. (1991). Treatment of eating-disordered patients with borderline and false-self/narcissistic disorders. In *Psychodynamic Treatment of Anorexia Nervosa and Bulimia*. New York: Guilford.

Joseph, B. (1982). Addiction to near death. *International Journal of Psycho-Analysis* 63:449–456.

Kalucy, R. S., Crisp, A. H., and Harding, B. (1977). A study of 56 families with anorexia nervosa. *British Journal of Medical Psychology* 50:381–395.

Kaplan, L. J. (1991). *Female Perversions: The Temptations of Emma Bovary*. New York: Nan A. Talese/Doubleday.

Kernberg, O. (1980). Foreword. In *Starving to Death in a Sea of Objects*, by J. Sours. New York: Jason Aronson.

Kornhaber, A. (1970). The stuffing syndrome. *Psychosomatics* 11: 580–584.

Krueger, D. (1988). Body self, psychological self, and bulimia: developmental and clinical considerations. In *Bulimia: Psychoanalytic Treatment and Theory*, ed. H. Schwartz. Madison, CT: International Universities Press.

Lacey, J. H. (1982). The bulimic syndrome at normal body weight: reflections on pathogenesis and clinical features. *International Journal of Eating Disorders* 2:59–66.

Laseque, C. (1873). On hysterical anorexia. *Medical Times Gazette* 2:265–226.

Lerner, H. D. (1986). Current developments in the psychoanalytic psychotherapy of anorexia nervosa and bulimia nervosa. *The Clinical Psychologist*, Spring, pp. 39–42.

―――― (1991). Masochism in subclinical eating disorders. In *Psychodynamic Treatment of Anorexia Nervosa and Bulimia*, ed. C. Johnson. New York: Guilford.

Lorand, S. (1943). Anorexia nervosa. *Psychosomatic Medicine* 5:282–292.

Lowenkopf, E. (1982). Anorexia nervosa: some nosological considerations. *Comprehensive Psychiatry* 23:233–240.

MacLeod, S. (1982). *The Art of Starvation: A Story of Anorexia and Survival*. New York: Schocken.

McDougall, J. (1989). *Theaters of the Body: A Psychoanalytic Approach to Psychosomatic Illness*. New York: W. W. Norton.

Mintz, I. L. (1980). Anorexia nervosa: the clinical syndrome and its dynamic implications. *Journal of the Medical Society of New Jersey* 77:33–339.

———— (1983a). An analytic approach to hospital and nursing care. In *Fear of Being Fat: The Treatment of Anorexia Nervosa and Bulimia*, ed. C. P. Wilson, C. Hogan, and I. Mintz. New York: Jason Aronson.

———— (1983b). Anorexia nervosa and bulimia in males. In *Fear of Being Fat: The Treatment of Anorexia Nervosa and Bulimia*, ed. C. P. Wilson, C. Hogan, and I. Mintz. New York: Jason Aronson.

———— (1983c). Psychoanalytic description: the clinical picture of anorexia nervosa and bulimia. In *Fear of Being Fat: The Treatment of Anorexia Nervosa and Bulimia*, ed. C. P. Wilson, C. Hogan, and I. Mintz. New York: Jason Aronson.

———— (1983d). Psychoanalytic therapy of severe anorexia: the case of Jeanette. In *Fear of Being Fat: The Treatment of Anorexia Nervosa and Bulimia*, ed. C. P. Wilson, C. Hogan, and I. Mintz. New York: Jason Aronson.

———— (1983e). The relationship between self-starvation and amenorrhea. In *Fear of Being Fat: The Treatment of Anorexia Nervosa and Bulimia*, ed. C. P. Wilson, C. Hogan, and I. Mintz. New York: Jason Aronson.

———— (1988). Self-destructive behavior in anorexia and bulimia. In *Bulimia: Psychoanalytic Treatment and Theory*, ed. H. Schwartz. Madison, CT: International Universities Press.

———— (1992a). Clinical vignettes. In *Psychodynamic Technique in the Treatment of the Eating Disorders*, ed. C. P. Wilson, C. Hogan, and I. Mintz. Northvale, NJ: Jason Aronson.

———— (1992b). A comparison between the analyst's view and the patient's diary. In *Psychodynamic Technique in the Treatment of Eating Disorders*, ed. C. P. Wilson, C. Hogan, and I. Mintz. Northvale, NJ: Jason Aronson.

Minuchin, S., Baker, L., Rosman, B. L., et al. (1975). A conceptual model of psychodynamic illness in children. *Archives of General Psychiatry* 32:1031–1035.

Minuchin, S., Rosman, B. L., and Baker, L. (1978). *Psychosomatic Families: Anorexia Nervosa in Context*. Cambridge, MA: Harvard University Press.

Mitchell, J. E., and Goff, G. (1984). Bulimia in male patients. *Psychosomatics* 25:909–913.

Mitchell, J. E., and Pyle, R. L. (1982). The bulimic syndrome in normal weight individuals: a review. *International Journal of Eating Disorders* 1:61–73.

Mitchell, J. E., Pyle, R. L., and Eckert, E. D. (1981). Frequency and duration of binge-eating episodes in patients with bulimia. *American Journal of Psychiatry* 136:835–836.

Modell, A. H. (1973). A narcissistic defence against affects and the illusion of self-sufficiency. *International Journal of Psycho-Analysis* 56:275–282.

Mogul, S. L. (1980). Asceticism in adolescence and anorexia nervosa. *Psychoanalytic Study of the Child* 35:155–175. New Haven: Yale University Press.

———— (1989). Sexuality, pregnancy, and parenting in anorexia nervosa. *Psychoanalysis and Eating Disorders*, ed. J. R. Bemporad and D. B. Herzog. New York: Guilford.

Morgan, H. G., and Russell, G. F. M. (1975). Value of family background and clinical features as predictors of long-term outcome in anorexia nervosa: four-year follow up study of 41 patients. *Psychological Medicine* 5:355–371.

Morton, R. (1694). *Phthisological; or a treatise of consumptions*. London: Smith and Walford.

Mushatt, C. (1982a). Anorexia nervosa: a psychoanalytic commentary. *International Journal of Eating Disorders* 2:51–60.

———— (1982b). Anorexia nervosa: a psychoanalytic commentary. *International Journal of Psychoanalytic Psychotherapy* 9:257–265.

———— (1992). Anorexia nervosa as an expression of ego defective development. In *Psychodynamic Technique in the Treatment of Eating Disorders*. Northvale, NJ: Jason Aronson.

Ogden, T. (1986). *The Matrix of the Mind: Object Relations and the Psychoanalytic Dialogue*. Northvale, NJ: Jason Aronson.

———— (1989). *The Primitive Edge of Experience*. Northvale, NJ: Jason Aronson.

Palazzoli, M. S. (1963). *L'Anoressia Mentale*. Milan: Feltrinelli. Republished as *Self-Starvation: From Individual to Family Therapy in the Treatment of Anorexia Nervosa*, trans. A. Pomerans. New York: Jason Aronson, 1974.

_____ (1988). *The Work of Mara Selvini Palazzoli*. Ed. M. Selvini. Northvale, NJ: Jason Aronson.

Pope, H. G., Jr., and Hudson, J. I. (1984). *New Hope for Binge Eaters*. New York: Harper & Row.

Pope, H. G., Jr., Hudson, J. I., and Jonas, J. M. (1983). Bulimia treated with imipramine: a placebo-controlled double-blind study. *American Journal of Psychiatry* 140:554–558.

Pyle, R. L., Mitchell, J. E., and Eckert, E. D. (1981). Bulimia: a report of 34 cases. *Journal of Clinical Psychiatry* 42:60–64.

Reiser, L. W. (1988). Love, work, and bulimia. In *Bulimia: Psychoanalytic Treatment and Theory*, ed. H. Schwartz. Madison, CT: International Universities Press.

_____ (1990). The oral triad and the bulimic quintet. Understanding the bulimic episode. *International Review of Psycho-Analysis* 17:239–247.

Riebel, L. K. (1990). The dropout problem in outpatient psychotherapy groups for bulimics and compulsive eaters. *Psychotherapy* 27:404–410.

Riese, H., and Rutan, J. S. (1992). Group therapy for eating disorders: a step-wise approach. *Group* 16:79–83.

Risen, S. E. (1988). Anorexia nervosa: theory and therapy—a new look at an old problem. *Journal of the American Psychoanalytic Association* 36:153–161.

Ritvo, S. (1980). The image and uses of the body in psychic conflict. With special reference to eating disorders in adolescence. *Psychoanalytic Study of the Child* 33:449–469. New Haven, CT: Yale University Press.

_____ (1988). Mothers, daughters, and eating disorders. In *In Honor of Jacob A. Arlow, M.D.*, ed. H. P. Blum. Madison, CT: International Universities Press.

Rizzuto, A. (1988). Transference, language, and affect in the treatment of bulimarexia. *International Journal of Psycho-Analysis* 69:369–387.

Rizzuto, A., Peterson, R. K., and Reed, M. (1981). The pathological sense of self in anorexia nervosa. In *Psychiatric Clinics of North America* 4:471–487.

Roberto, L. G. (1993). Eating disorders as family secrets. In *Secrets in Families and Family Therapy*, ed. E. Imber-Black. New York: W. W. Norton.

Root, M. P. P., Fallon, P., and Friedrich, W. N. (1986). *Bulimia: A Systems Approach to Treatment*. New York: W. W. Norton.

Russell, G. (1979). Bulimia nervosa: an ominous variant of anorexia nervosa. *Psychological Medicine* 9:429–448.

Sacksteder, J. L. (1989a). Personalization as an aspect of the process of change in anorexia nervosa. In *The Facilitating Environment: Clinical Applications of Winnicott's Theory*, ed. G. M. Fromm and B. L. Smith. Madison, CT: International Universities Press.

––––––– (1989b). Psychosomatic dissociation and the false self development in anorexia nervosa. In *The Facilitating Environment: Clinical Applications of Winnicott's Theory*, ed. G. M. Fromm and B. L. Smith. Madison, CT: International Universities Press.

––––––– (1989c). Sadomasochistic relatedness to the body in anorexia nervosa. In *Masochism: The Treatment of Self-Inflicted Suffering*, ed. J. Montgomery and A. Grief. Madison, CT: International Universities Press.

Sands, S. (1989). Eating disorders and female development: a self-psychological perspective. In *Dimensions of Self-Experience*, ed. A. Goldberg. Hillsdale, NJ: Analytic Press.

––––––– (1991). Bulimia, dissociation, and empathy: a self-psychological view. In *Psychodynamic Treatment of Anorexia Nervosa and Bulimia*, ed. C. Johnson. New York: Guilford.

Schneider, J. A. (1991). Gender identity issues in male bulimia nervosa. In *Psychodynamic Treatment of Anorexia Nervosa and Bulimia*, ed. C. Johnson. New York: Guilford.

Schwartz, D. M., Thompson, M. G., and Johnson, C. L. (1982). Anorexia nervosa and bulimia: the socio-cultural context. *International Journal of Eating Disorders* 1:20–36.

Schwartz, H. (1988). Bulimia: psychoanalytic perspectives. In *Bulimia: Psychoanalytic Treatment and Theory*. Madison, CT: International Universities Press.

Seton, P. (1972). Anorexia nervosa and affect boundaries in a male college student: a case report. Paper presented at the Western New England Psychoanalytic Society, New Haven, CT, Fall.

Simpson, M. (1973). Female genital self-mutilation. *Archives of General Psychiatry* 29:808–810.

Sours, J. (1974). The anorexia nervosa syndrome. *International Journal of Psycho-Analysis* 55:567–576.

_____ (1980). *Starving to Death in a Sea of Objects: The Anorexia Nervosa Syndrome.* New York: Jason Aronson.

_____ (1981). Depression and the anorexia nervosa syndrome. *Psychiatric Clinics of North America* 4:145–148.

Sperling, M. (1955). Psychosis and psychosomatic illness. *International Journal of Psycho-Analysis* 36:320–327. Also in *Psychosomatic Disorders in Childhood.* New York: Jason Aronson, 1978.

Sprince, M. P. (1984). Early psychic disturbances in anorexic and bulimic patients as reflected in the psychoanalytic process. *Journal of Child Psychotherapy* 10:199–215.

_____ (1988). Experiencing and recovering transitional space in the analytic treatment of anorexia nervosa and bulimia. In *Bulimia: Psychoanalytic Treatment and Theory,* ed. H. J. Schwartz, pp. 73–88. Madison, CT: International Universities Press.

_____ (1989). Experiencing and recovering transitional space. In *Dimensions of Self Experience,* vol. 5 of *Progress in Self Psychology,* ed. A. Goldberg. Hillsdale, NJ: Analytic Press.

Stern, S. (1986). The dynamics of clinical management in the treatment of anorexia nervosa and bulimia: an organizing theory. *International Journal of Eating Disorders* 5:233–254.

Stierlin, H., and Weber, G. (1989). *Unlocking the Family Door: A Systemic Approach to the Understanding and Treatment of Anorexia Nervosa.* New York: Brunner/Mazel.

Story, R. I. (1990). The psychotherapy of anorexia nervosa in the light of Winnicott's concepts. *The Austen Riggs Center Review* 2:4–6.

Strangler, R. S., and Printz, A. M. (1980). *D.S.M. III* psychiatry diagnosis in a university population. *American Journal of Psychiatry* 137:937–940.

Strober, M. (1981). The significance of bulimia in juvenile anorexia nervosa: an exploration of possible etiologic factors. *International Journal of Eating Disorders* 1:28–43.

Strober, M., and Yager, J. (1984). A developmental perspective on the treatment of anorexia nervosa in adolescents. In *The Handbook of Psychotherapy for Anorexia and Bulimia,* ed. D. Garner and P. Garfinkel. New York: Guilford.

Sugarman, A. (1991). Bulimia: a displacement from psychological self to body self. In *Psychodynamic Treatment of Anorexia and Bulimia,* ed. C. Johnson. New York: Guilford.

Sugarman, A., and Kurash, C. (1982). The body as a transitional object in bulimia. *International Journal of Eating Disorders* 1:57–67.

Sugarman, A., and Quinlan, D. (1981). *Anorexia Nervosa.* Trans. G. Brydone. New York: International Universities Press.

Surrey, J. L. (1985). Colloquium: eating patterns as a reflection of women's development. In *Work in Progress,* No. 83–06. Wellesley, MA: Stone Center for Developmental Services and Studies.

Swift, W. J. (1991). Bruch revisited: the role of interpretation of transference and resistance in the psychotherapy of eating disorders. In *Psychodynamic Treatment of Anorexia Nervosa and Bulimia,* ed. C. Johnson. New York: Guilford.

Swift, W. J., and Letven, R. (1984). Bulimia and the basic fault: a psychoanalytic interpretation of the binge-vomiting syndrome. *Journal of the American Academy of Child Psychiatry* 23:489–497.

Swift, W. J., and Stern, S. (1982). The psychodynamic diversity of anorexia nervosa. *The International Journal of Eating Disorders* 2:17–35.

Thomä, H. (1967). *Anorexia Nervosa.* New York: International Universities Press.

———— (1977). On the psychotherapy of patients with anorexia nervosa. *Bulletin of the Menninger Clinic* 41:437–452.

Thompson, M. G., and Schwartz, D. M. (1982). Life adjustment of women with anorexia nervosa and anorexic-like behavior. *International Journal of Eating Disorders* 1:47–60.

Thompson, R. A., and Sherman, R. T. (1989). Therapist errors in treating eating disorders: relationship and process. *Psychotherapy* 26:62–68.

Tustin, F. (1959). Anorexia nervosa in an adolescent girl. *British Journal of Medical Psychology* 31:184–200.

Vandereycken, W., and Pierloot, P. (1983). The significance of subclassification in anorexia nervosa: a comparative study of clinical features in 141 patients. *Psychological Medicine* 13:543–549.

Vanderlinden, J., Norre, J., and Vandereycken, W. (1992). *A Practical Guide to the Treatment of Bulimia Nervosa.* New York: Brunner/Mazel.

Waller, J. V., Kaufman, M. R., and Deutsch, F. (1940). Anorexia nervosa: a psychosomatic entity. *Psychosomatic Medicine* 2:3–16.

Wennik-Kaplan, R. (1990). The question of psychogenicity in anorexic amenorrhea: a study of maternal identification conflict. Ph.D. dissertation. New York University School of Social Work.

Wilson, C. P. (1983a). Introduction. In *Fear of Being Fat: The Treatment of Anorexia Nervosa and Bulimia*, ed. C. P. Wilson, C. Hogan, and I. Mintz. New York: Jason Aronson.

_____ (1983b). The family psychological profile and its therapeutic implications. In *Fear of Being Fat: The Treatment of Anorexia Nervosa and Bulimia*, ed. C. P. Wilson, C. Hogan, and I. Mintz. New York: Jason Aronson.

_____ (1988). Bulimic equivalents. In *Bulimia: Psychoanalytic Treatment and Theory*, ed. H. Schwartz. Madison, CT: International Universities Press.

_____ (1990). On beginning analysis with patients with eating disorders. In *On Beginning Analysis*, ed. T. J. Jacobs and A. Rothstein. Madison, CT: International Universities Press.

Wilson, C. P., and Mintz, I. (1982). Abstaining and bulimic anorexics: two sides of the same coin. *Primary Care* 9:517–530.

Wolf, N. (1991). *The Beauty Myth: How Images of Beauty Are Used Against Women*. New York: William Morrow.

Woodall, C. (1987). The body as a transitional object in bulimia: a critique of the concept. *Adolescent Psychiatry* 14:179–184.

Wooley, S. C. (1991). Uses of countertransference in the treatment of eating disorders: a gender perspective. In *Psychodynamic Treatment of Anorexia Nervosa and Bulimia*, ed. C. Johnson. New York: Guilford.

Yager, J. (1985). The outpatient treatment of bulimia. *Bulletin of the Menninger Clinic* 49:203–236.

Yager, J., Landsverk, J., and Edelstein, C. K., (1987). A 20-month follow-up study of 628 women with eating disorders, I: course and severity. *American Journal of Psychiatry* 144:1172–1177.

Zerbe, K. (1992). Eating disorders in the 1990s: clinical challenges and treatment implications. *Bulletin of the Menninger Clinic* 56:167–187.

Credits

261

Index